Police State

Key Concepts in Political Science

GENERAL EDITOR: Leonard Schapiro
EXECUTIVE EDITOR: Peter Calvert

Other titles in the same series include:

ALREADY PUBLISHED

IN PREPARATION

Police State

Brian Chapman
University of Manchester

Macmillan

Published in the United States of America in 1970
by Praeger Publishers Inc.

This edition published in 1971 by
MACMILLAN AND CO LTD
London and Basingstoke
Associated companies in New York Toronto
Dublin Melbourne Johannesburg and Madras

SBN 333 11355 1 (paper cover)

Printed in Great Britain by
RICHARD CLAY (THE CHAUCER PRESS), LTD
Bungay Suffolk

Not for sale in the U.S.A.

Contents

'Key Concepts'
an Introductory Note

Political concepts are part of our daily speech—we abuse 'bureaucracy' and praise 'democracy', welcome or recoil from 'revolution'. Emotive words such as 'equality', 'dictatorship', 'élite' or even 'power' can often, by the very passions which they raise, obscure a proper understanding of the sense in which they are, or should be, or should not be, or have been used. Confucius regarded the 'rectification of names' as the first task of government. 'If names are not correct, language will not be in accordance with the truth of things', and this in time would lead to the end of justice, to anarchy and to war. One could with some truth point out that the attempts hitherto by governments to enforce their own quaint meanings on words have not been conspicuous for their success in the advancement of justice. 'Rectification of names' there must certainly be: but most of us would prefer such rectification to take place in the free debate of the university, in the competitive arena of the pages of the book or journal.

Analysis of commonly used political terms, their reassessment or their 'rectification', is, of course, normal activity in the political science departments of our universities. The idea of this series was indeed born in the course of discussion between a few university teachers of political science, of whom Professor S. E. Finer of Manchester University was one. It occurred to us that a series of short books, discussing the 'Key Concepts' in political science would serve two purposes. In universities these books could provide the kind of brief political texts which might be of assistance to students in gaining a fuller understanding of the terms which they were constantly using. But we also hoped that outside the universities there exists a reading public which has the time, the curiosity and the inclination to pause to reflect on some of those words and ideas which are so often taken for granted. Perhaps even 'that insidious and crafty animal', as Adam Smith described the politician and statesman, will occasionally derive some pleasure or even profit from the more leisurely analysis which academic study can afford, and which a busy life in the practice of politics often denies.

It has been very far from the minds of those who have been concerned in planning and bringing into being the 'Key Concepts' series to try and impose (as if that were possible!) any uniform pattern on the authors who have contributed, or will contribute, to it. I, for one, hope that each author will, in his own individual manner, seek and find the best way of helping us to a fuller understanding of the concept which he has chosen to analyse. But whatever form the individual exposition may take, there are, I believe, three aspects of illumination which we can confidently expect from each volume in this series. First, we can look for some examination of the history of the concept, and of its evolution against a changing social and political background. I believe, as many do who are concerned with the study of political science, that it is primarily in history that the explanation must be sought for many of the perplexing problems of political analysis and judgement which beset us today. Second, there is the semantic aspect. To look in depth at a 'key concept' necessarily entails a study of the name which attached itself to it; of the different ways in which, and the different purposes for which, the name was used; of the way in which in the course of history·the same name was applied to several concepts, or several names were applied to one and the same concept; and, indeed, of the changes which the same concept, or what appears to be the same concept, has undergone in the course of time. This analysis will usually require a searching examination of the relevant literature in order to assess the present stage of scholarship in each particular field. And thirdly, I hope that the reader of each volume in this series will be able to decide for himself what the proper and valid use should be of a familiar term in politics, and will gain, as it were, from each volume a sharper and better-tempered tool of political analysis.

There are many today who would disagree with Bismarck's view that politics can never be an exact science. I express no opinion on this much debated question. But all of us who are students of politics—and our numbers both inside and outside the universities continue to grow—will be the better for knowing what precisely we mean when we use a common political term.

London School of Economics
and Political Science

Leonard Schapiro
General Editor

1/The Origins of the Term

The term 'police state' has been so misunderstood by English-speaking people that only a plain historical account of its origins will enable the reader properly to understand what follows in later chapters of this study. The misunderstanding has arisen because the word 'police' has actually two senses, whereas we normally only use it in one. This misunderstanding became greater when the phrase 'police state', a literal translation of the German *Polizeistaat*, entered common English usage in the late 1930s. It then acquired the connotations with which we are familiar, and the real sense of the original was lost. We will see that we have two potent sources of confusion: an original failure to distinguish between two separable ideas, and a contemporary failure to distinguish between different notions of the state. The term police state has therefore come to be used indiscriminately to lump together three different types of state, which have certain features in common but which when analysed are intrinsically very different in their natures. This first chapter will attempt to describe the origins and philosophy of the first of these types, the 'traditional police state'.

To do so we must turn back to Roman law. The Romans took over from the Greeks the term *politeia*, which became latinized as *politia*. It was a derivative from the Greek word for city, *polis*, and the English words 'politics' and 'policy' come from this same root. The term politeia was a comprehensive one, touching on all matters affecting the survival and welfare of the inhabitants of the city. It comprised within itself the whole notion of 'the art of governing the city'. In Greek times this concept was inseparable from the law governing the institutions of the city state. Plato and Aristotle regarded the officials responsible for 'the police' as being invested with the ultimate responsibility for ensuring the safety of the republic. This involved the power to regulate the affairs of the city in the general interest of public order, security, morality, food supplies and welfare. It also involved having at the disposal of the public authority a force of men, the guardians of the law, to ensure that the regulations were obeyed, with powers to keep order in the streets, to ensure fair trading in the markets and to suppress scandalous behaviour. These guardians had summary powers of punishment, but serious offences against the republic had to be referred to courts of higher instance.

Thus, a distinction can already be observed. On the one hand a public authority with legal power to organize the republic in the interests of the safety and welfare of the population; and, on the other hand, a body of men empowered to enforce these rules of conduct, if necessary by the use of physical force.

This distinction became more marked in Roman times. The juridical theory underlying the authority of the emperor was that he incarnated the *imperium* of the state; this imperium had originally resided in the people as a whole, but by the theoretical passage of a mythical *lex regia* the people had assigned its sovereignty to the emperor. It was vested in him as a public authority, not as an individual, and Roman law, at least until Justinian's time, was careful to maintain this distinction between the public and private personalities of the emperor. The imperium underlay all the authority of the state, and was the legal foundation for all acts of power.

But power (*potestas*) itself consisted of two elements, which are still implicit in the meaning attached to the word today. First, power meant the legal authority to regulate conduct, to issue binding instructions, to promulgate edicts; second, it meant the legal possession of the means of physical coercion, the instruments to force, to require, to compel. Sovereignty meant the absolute uncontrolled and uncontrollable authority of the state and it comprised all aspects of power in both senses. The sovereign authority was the ultimate legal basis for all legislation, all judicial pronouncements, all penalties, all policy, all acts of state. Subordinate to it, but an integral part of it, was the police 'power' and the police 'force'. All matters of municipal, as opposed to military, concern were in the last resort the responsibility of the police authority relying upon the coercive resources of the police force.

Hence, although Roman law accepted distinctive functions for different state institutions, the police power was regarded as lying at the very heart of state authority. The essence of government is the power to prescribe the permitted limits of public and private behaviour, and to formulate them into legal norms. The fundamental right of the state, which distinguishes it from all other forms of association, is the power to coerce, if necessary by recourse to physical force. The police power, as an emanation of sovereignty, was the basis of the practical authority of the state.

This doctrine was accurately reflected in the administrative institutions of the empire. The *praefectus urbi*, the 'prefect of the city', exercised the police powers and also controlled the police force. He had the authority to impose rules to control public order, fire risks, public buildings, religious observances, public and private meetings, the activities of prostitutes, beggars and foreigners, and generally to safeguard the health, safety and morality of the population. To enforce the regulations he made under his police authority, the prefect had at his disposal fourteen magistrates, the *curatores urbis*, each responsible for a district of the city; they, in turn were assisted by *vigiles* who patrolled the streets, *stationarii*, residents of a city block, and *lictores*, who acted as the magistrates' enforcement officers. Thus, the prefect of the city exercised the police powers and controlled the police force at one and the same time.

This system was extended from Rome to all the principal cities of the empire. It disappeared without trace as the Roman Empire crumbled before the attacks of the barbarians. During the long night of the Dark Ages the most elementary concepts of Roman law were lost in western Europe, as well as the sophisticated administrative structures of the old empire. Europe reverted to the most primitive forms of government, and clan loyalties or personal allegiance to a chieftain became the sole source of authority. The distinctive nature of the police power was lost, and the distinctive roles of administrator, soldier and judge were confused together in one person.

Traces of the word *policie* or *politie* can be found in medieval French, used in the sense of maintaining order in the city, and also in the more general sense of 'government'. In the early Middle Ages we can distinguish royal, seigneurial and municipal officers vying with each other to bring under their own jurisdiction the control of the streets, the supervision of markets, and the protection of life and property. It was not, however, until Francis I (1494–1547) of France that we can clearly distinguish a recognizable modern police force. This force, the precursor of the modern *Gendarmerie* (*Gens d'Armes*), was placed under the control of *prévôts de maréchaux*, and comprised lieutenants and archers, although even then it was essentially a military force for policing the countryside and highways, rather than a public authority with police 'powers'.

But by now the treasures of Roman law had been rediscovered, and the lessons taught in the universities of Bologna and Padova received a ready hearing in the universities of Paris, Cologne and Leipzig. The new jurists resurrected the mythical lex regia of Roman law, and argued that the imperium belonged to the prince; by an ingenious use of the Roman law of property they identified this imperium with an individual's private property. The state was an 'estate' owned by the monarch, and only he could use it, transmit it to his heirs, or otherwise limit or dispose of it. The Roman jurists' careful distinction between the emperor's private and public personalities was conveniently forgotten. Indeed, the argument lay at the very heart of the constitutional doctrine of absolute monarchy which was now being shaped. Police, law and government were all emanations of the prince's sovereignty, and as such part of the very nature of the state. This theory provided the justification for encroachments on feudal, aristocratic, municipal and guild rights, and the slow progress of rationalization and nationalization from which emerged the modern state.

In this new world the new jurists also taught the importance of distinguishing between the different functions of the state. Financial administration, justice, defence and foreign affairs were all distinguishable state functions in most European countries by the end of the seventeenth century. The word 'police' began to take on the connotations of internal administration, welfare, protection, and, in the more modern sense, surveillance. In 1667 Louis XIV created a special post of *lieutenant de police* in Paris with jurisdiction over the city and county of Paris. The scope of the authority vested in the position can be traced in administrative acts: the formation of standing patrols, the regulation of food supplies, street lighting, the collection of household refuse, the closing of the infamous *Cour de Miracles*, traffic control, street cleaning, fire precautions, the foundation and regulation of a Paris stock exchange, the regulation of prostitution, the appointment of concierges, and, less publicly promulgated, the systematic penetration of all levels of society by spies and informers.

The new jurists, the prestige of France, and the single-minded genius of the electors of Brandenburg, took these ideas across the Rhine, and led to the first 'police state' in Europe. The Polizeistaat as it was developed in Prussia in the eighteenth century was the product of economic, social and military policies. Mercantilism involved the regulation of the economy to promote the common good, the common good being not only the welfare of the individual but also the strength of the state. The municipal economies of medieval times came to be replaced by territorial economies, and mercantilism involved the creation of a balanced national economy, a favourable balance of trade, a buoyant national revenue and the means of war under state control.

This economic doctrine was reinforced by social and dynastic considerations. The devastation of the Thirty Years War in Europe predisposed large sections of the population of central Europe to prefer order to liberty, and protection to freedom. The dynastic interests of rulers favoured the creation of strong, internally stable and strictly disciplined states. In a Hobbesian world political survival seemed to be dependent on military strength placed at the service of the state.

As we move further into the eighteenth century the principles of the Enlightenment come to add a new element to the thinking behind the development of the modern state. If these principles were interpreted in a special way, they could be used to justify the benevolent despotism of the prince. Both sides could agree on the virtues of religious toleration, the dismantling of aristocratic and municipal privilege, and the introduction into government of general principles of law. The Reformation had strengthened the authority of the state over the churches, and both the new jurists and Christian thinkers could concur on the traditional Christian's duty to obey constituted authority.

The first Polizeistaat was, therefore, dedicated to three purposes: the protection of the population, the welfare of the state and its citizens, and the improvement of society. The reforms of Frederick William of Prussia (1620–88) and his successors were designed to create a tightly organized and rigorously administered state which could meet these different needs. The feudal powers of the princelings were whittled away, a modern army—organized on strict hierarchical lines—was created, and a new type of bureaucratic system was introduced. The old aristocracy, dispossessed of its political power, moved into the army, and made it the anchor and the guardian of the state. The new bureaucracy, drawn from the ranks of the middle class and entirely dependent on the will of the prince, devoted its efforts to building up an administrative system to provide the infrastructure of a strong, centralized and hierarchically organized state. Its role was to establish what we would now call a mobilization system, and it developed strict rules for the proper management of the economy, for the internal security and provisioning of the population, and for the prudent administration of public affairs.

The new school of Prussian jurists, the Cameralists, provided the juridical justification for this process and rationalized the entire method of organizing public offices and training the new bureaucrats. With the reforms of Frederick II (1712–86) entry to the public service was opened to merit rather than birth, and senior bureaucrats could only be appointed if they possessed a university degree in 'Cameralistics', and this required knowledge of agricultural economics, estate management, financial management, administrative law and administrative science (police).

The internal structure of the administration was organized on hierarchical lines, administrative business being divided rationally between departments, and subordinate offices strictly subject to the control of the next in line. Government offices were created in the provinces to conduct the state's local business and to supervise the work of the local authorities on behalf of the state. At the apex of this pyramid stood the prince who manipulated this bureaucratic corps—obedient, disciplined, responsive and responsible—as a general might deploy his troops. The Prussian army was to protect the integrity of the state, and to provide the state with a disciplined force when a forward policy demanded aggression. The civil service was to protect the internal peace of the country, to develop its internal economy, to provide law and order and to support the army.

The philosophy of this Polizeistaat, as expounded by the Cameralists, was as important as the institutional framework. The state had to be all-powerful since, in the last resort, its welfare must transcend the individual and particular interests of individuals within the state. Citizens who were properly aware of this would always recognize that the state must have the last word, even at the cost of injury or injustice to themselves, since the fundamental concern of all citizens was the protection and integrity of the state. Without the state all would be lost. The will of the state was embodied in the person of the prince, but the prince acted for the state and not simply for his own private benefit, and to that extent he was the servant of the state as were all other citizens. The will of the prince was governed by the ultimate *raison d'état*, and it was his burden to interpret what that had to be.

This doctrine had two important constitutional effects. First, political and administrative authority—legislation and regulation—were fused, and both the legislative function and the administrative process were regarded as one aspect of the police power of the state. Second, in the judical process the private citizen could have no legitimate way to protect his interests against those higher interests of the state. An appeal against the decision of a state authority could always be allowed as a matter of grace by an administrative superior, but the ordinary courts could have no jurisdiction in administrative and political matters. The courts were not equipped to understand and interpret the real interests of the state, and they could therefore have no jurisdiction to question the reasons for its policies or actions.

The Polizeistaat was not, however, a state of arbitrary rule. Officials were themselves required to act according to well-defined rules, subject to precise limits, and within prescribed powers. They operated within the laws of the state and the regulations of the administration, and they were personally liable for breaches of the law. It was an official's superior's duty to determine whether or not a breach of the law had occurred, and whether or not the state should give redress for an official's actions. The state's ultimate discretion could not be bound by its own instruments, and its interests could not be determined by any body other than itself. But one of the fundamental interests of the state was in the equity of its operations and in the maintenance of a proper ethical relationship between itself and its citizens.

Nor was the Polizeistaat a state devoted to repression. Individuals were subordinated to the greater good of the state, but the welfare of the state was also intrinsically that of its citizens. The state had a higher purpose, and the single directing will was the means whereby this could be achieved.

In institutional terms this meant that everything relating to internal public law, with the exception of purely financial, military and judicial matters, belonged to the minister of the interior, subject to the overriding power of the king. The minister, and his subordinates, were the 'police' authorities, that is, those concerned with maintaining the structure, health and protection of society. In the words of the General Ordinance of 1808, police authorities were

> . . . to care for the general welfare of our [the king's] loyal subjects from the negative, as well as from the positive, point of view. They are not so much entitled as in duty bound, not only to avoid and ward off all which could bring danger and disadvantage to the state and its citizens and to maintain the institutions necessary to the preservation of public peace, security and order, but also to ensure that the general welfare is promoted and increased, and that every citizen has the opportunity to develop his abilities and his powers from a moral and physical point of view, and, within the limits of the law, to employ them in the manner most beneficial to him.

There are some striking parallels between this state philosophy and those of some contemporary states, and it is as well to note at this stage that the first police state had at its heart the desire to create a mobilization system, a development economy and a welfare state.

2/The Traditional Police State

The traditional police state in its highest form also involved the development and rationalization of the official police forces with which we associate the concept today. The intellectual stimulus for the creation of the Polizeistaat came from the Prussian Cameralists, and the organizing genius for its foundation from Frederick William and Frederick II of Prussia, but the most deliberate, sustained and systematic attempt to create a modern state apparatus based not only on the extensive use of police powers, but also on the use of police forces as the country's supervisory censor, was made by Joseph II (1741–90) of Austria. It was he who saw the importance of public opinion. The concomitant need to control it led to the police becoming a unique state apparat with a general and overriding competence for the supervision of government. (Later, in his turn, Fouché, in post-revolutionary France, accepted this view and gave to the police a genuinely ideological *raison d'être*.)

Joseph II saw himself as the stern but solicitous father of his people. For him the state was intended to serve the greatest good of the greatest number, (a phrase later famous in English philosophy, under very different auspices). He swept away old-fashioned and unmethodical methods of government and replaced them according to the models he adopted from his mentor, Frederick II of Prussia. In his ten-year reign he issued 6,000 decrees, and over 1,147 folio pages of instructions. He abolished the privileged feudal and ecclesiastical courts and jurisdictions, and replaced them with an organized legal system freed from the restraints and peculiarities of customary law and local precedents. He promulgated new civil, property and criminal codes and modernized criminal law procedures. He increased personal freedom, allowed divorce, encouraged commerce, freed estates from the ancient law of primogeniture, abolished the death penalty, and placed all citizens on an equal footing before the law. He regulated relations between the different bodies within the state and reformed the relations between the Church and state. He encouraged education as being of benefit to the state, and he looked forward to the time when with its help citizens would develop a natural maturity and responsibility which could justify a greater increase in personal liberty.

Following the Prussian model, he relied for the success of this great series of reforms on the establishment of an honest, educated and efficient bureaucracy. He encouraged civil servants to attend university to perfect their training, and expected from each official a personal report about his life and progress every six months. He expected his officials to devote themselves entirely to the interests of the state, and to be without outside concerns, He insisted on complete impartiality and integrity on the part of all officials in the conduct of their official business and in their private lives: 'in the business of the State personal inclinations should not have the slightest influence; everybody must give his best and carry out his duties regardless of rank or ceremony'.[1] He drove his officials hard, but as a recompense he improved and formalized their conditions of service, created a proper career structure for them, and set up an organized pension scheme.

Joseph was much more conscious than Frederick II of the importance of public opinion. He was always accessible to his subjects, and dealt with and, indeed, encouraged complaints. He would personally follow up reported abuses, and he drove himself, as he drove his officials, to be upright, compassionate and equitable.

He was, however, a man of little trust, and underlying his determined enlightenment there lay a profoundly pessimistic view of the nature of men and their capacity to be virtuous. He doubted the good faith of his officials, and he doubted the good

sense of public opinion. He was also very conscious of his vulnerability on two fronts. His own reforms, following those made by
his mother Maria Theresa, clearly alienated all the traditional
classes whose privileges were being whittled away. Moreover, he
was also faced with a very modern phenomenon, the emergence
of secret societies which challenged the foundations of the state.
And their members were to be found not in the mobs of the
cities, which could be handled by cavalry and peasant soldiery,
but in the intellectual, bureaucratic and governing circles upon
which he had to depend for the effectiveness of his reforms.

By the time Joseph II came to the throne the original secret
society dedicated to the principles of the Enlightenment, the
Masons, had for the most part declined into ineptitude and even
obscurantism. It had always had an ambiguous position in
society, and the ordinary lodges had been superseded as a radical force by the more militant members of the 'Strict Observance' lodges. These in their turn, however, were outflanked by
the foundation of the order of *Illuminati* in 1776 by Adam
Weishaupt at Ingolstadt.[2] This order was the model upon which
most of the revolutionary secret societies of the next century and
a half were to be based. Its members were pledged to fight
tyranny and oppression—which in concrete terms meant royal
absolutism—feudal privilege and supernatural religion. Its institutional structure was borrowed partly from the Jesuits, partly
from 'Strict Observance' Masonry. It claimed possession of exclusive secrets, had an elaborate and secret initiation ceremony,
a strictly organized hierarchy, and demanded absolute obedience, secrecy and discipline of all its adherents. Its ordinance
on secrecy could be adopted by any future conspiratorial group:

> The Order will seek to remain clandestine as much as
> possible, for whatever is secret and hidden has a special
> attraction for men: it attracts the interests of outsiders
> and enhances the loyalty of insiders. It gives superiors a
> special opportunity to judge the conduct of men in the

lower grades under circumstances where they do not know they are being observed. It also gives the order some protection from the impertinent curiosity of spies. Its noble purpose can be thwarted less easily, and any thirst for power which may exist on the part of superiors can be repressed more easily.

Instruction for its adherents went on in small tutorial groups, self-examination in accordance with detailed questionnaires was required, and reports on the qualities of new members and novices were a part of normal duties.[3]

It had an essentially liberal, upper- and middle-class and intellectual membership which has been estimated as between two and four thousand.[4] Its members had much in common with comparable groups known to the police in later generations. They were sincerely devoted to the welfare of the masses for whom they simultaneously felt contempt, and they had an inflated sense of their own importance, reinforced by their sense of belonging to a clandestine organization operating outside the law. The order attracted the usual potpourri of political conspiracies:

> . . . fanatical idealists who relished the dangerous struggle of the children of light against the forces of darkness; adventurers who delighted in matching their wits against an inquisitorial police; power hungry leaders who manipulated a docile body of followers through command, espionage, blackmail, and dire threats against traitors; and opportunists who could hope, before the order became utterly disreputable, that their careers would be fostered by the cliquish solidarity for which the order was notable.[5]

Joseph II undoubtedly overestimated the danger and importance of the Illuminati. They did not in fact operate as a single group under central direction, and there is no evidence that they ever followed a specific political programme, even though their later sympathy with the French invader during the revolutionary wars suggested a penchant for treason. But they did deliberately foster the interests of their own members, and attempt to place them in strategic positions, and since the majority of the membership came from princes, priests, officers, lawyers, doctors and merchants they represented an insidious force in the heart of society and the state. The supreme chancellor for the Hapsburg monarchy, Count Leopold Kolowrat, the eminent Viennese professor Joseph von Sonnenfels, the president of the Commission for Education, Gottfried van Swieten, the prominent diplomat Count Johann Cobenzl, and the favourite poet Alxinger were all Illuminati. Yet they and men like them in strategic state positions were those on whom Joseph had to rely for the success of his reforms.

Joseph therefore developed a highly complex and all-pervasive police system to observe the calibre and work of his officials, and to keep strategic offices under constant surveillance. His district commissioners were given minute instructions as to what they should observe. They were to report on the keeping of registers, on the behaviour and public utterances of priests, on the conditions of barracks, schools, hospitals, roads and private habitations. Enquiries were to be made to ensure that trade was properly regulated. General reports were to be made on the condition of the population and on the provision of assistance for the poor, alcoholics, unmarried mothers and foundlings.

The official police forces were centralized, and removed from the jurisdiction of the provincial governors. Special police commissioners, simply attached to the governors' offices, were appointed instead, and they reported directly to the minister of the interior in Vienna. The minister in his turn had direct and immediate access to Joseph himself, and this new police organization was underpinned by a secret police operating according to the emperor's most secret instructions. It was not, of course, the first time that a government had set up a secret police network, but Joseph's new system was the first of the modern age in its systematic penetration of all classes of society, and in the lavishness of its resources. It was also modern in that it was not primarily created to watch for court intrigues or desperate revolutionaries, but in order to maintain surveillance of the official classes, the army, the bureaucracy, the judges and the clergy.[6]

The confidential instructions which the emperor gave to his secret police force were to be known only to the most senior police officials and to the provincial governors. The employment of secret police agents was an official state secret, and the agents were to operate under the cloak of the official police service. The secret instructions made it quite explicit that continual surveillance should be maintained on officials, the clergy and army officers. Officials were to be watched to see whether they received bribes, whether they corresponded with relatives abroad, and whether they communicated official secrets to suspicious strangers. Army officers were watched to see whether they had any communication with foreign powers, and in this field the secret police acted as the counter-intelligence service. The clergy, whom Joseph rightly suspected as potential dissidents in a privileged position as 'opinion-leaders', were particularly marked out for strict supervision to ensure that they did not disseminate views contrary to the interests of the state or hostile to the emperor.

The secret police were also expected to keep a more general watch on the state of the nation. The agents were encouraged to investigate and report on the activities of other groups. To reinforce his supervision of the official classes Joseph expected the secret police to find out to what extent the people were satisfied with their treatment, and the frontier police were discreetly to examine private correspondence in order to track down disloyal officials. They were also required to report on the public standing of the emperor and his government, to identify malcontents, and to discover whether money was being exported, the laws of the land neglected or 'whether anything else is done to the prejudice of the State'. The secret police were also to check on foreigners, spies and forgers, and to report immediately if known agitators or suspected persons passed through the territory or moved towards Vienna.

The second part of the emperor's instructions to the secret police set out the means of operating the system and the methods to be used. An army of informers was recruited by selected police agents, who paid for information received. The spies were drawn from all levels of society, and no one was in too lowly a position to be useful: servants, messengers, drivers or porters; colleagues, neighbours and business contacts were recruited where necessary. The whole system amounted to a veritable charter for a society watched as well as guarded by the police service, with public opinion under the continual surveillance of secret police agents. This version of the traditional police state combined paternalism, autocracy and enlightenment on the one hand, with secret police, constant surveillance and paid informers on the other.

It is important to remember that the traditional police state was based on the best motives. Joseph wished to modernize his state, to encourage trade, to provide a corps of honest, dedicated and hard-working officials responsive ultimately to public demands. He saw his subjects as children, still unable properly to reason or to understand, and in need of guidance. He favoured no class, but expected all men to be like him and devote themselves to the betterment of their country. But as far as he understood human nature he doubted the natural intelligence, integrity, dynamism and selflessness of his subjects. He created a police system to ensure the integrity of the state and to ensure the best performance of their duties by his subjects. He did not wish to tyrannize his people; he wished to free them, by supervision, of the danger of falling prey to agitators, demagogues and revolutionaries. He wished to free them from their slavery of ignorance, ingenuousness and immaturity; and to do so he put them under the tutelage of an all-pervasive police. The prince was the guardian of the state, the police his agents.

This highly conservative and currently unfashionable view that there are certain people or groups in society who know better than others what is worth preserving or improving was carried still further by that great architect of police power and theorist of an ideology of the police, Fouché, Duc d'Otranto, minister of police to Napoleon in post-revolutionary France (1759–1820).

Unlike the kings of Prussia, the kings of France in the eighteenth century had been unsuccessful in centralizing and modernizing the administrative structure of the country. The internal structure of pre-revolutionary France was so decentralized, with so many sources of competing power, that policing, in the English sense of the word, was unsystematic, ineffective and haphazard. The royal corps of men at arms, the Gendarmerie, provided for the safety of the highways, and local communities provided for their own security according to traditional laws and customs. But most eighteenth-century literature on the subject stresses the inability of the police adequately to maintain public order, health or morality in the densely populated quarters of Paris, from which the revolutionary mobs were eventually to come.

This lack of concern with the day-to-day security of the population was emphasized by the distinction which was made in France between the 'low police', which concerned itself with mundane matters such as controlling markets, public sanitation and prostitutes; and the 'high police', which was the police service concerned with plots, and which had a general warrant to spy at will in all quarters of the city and at all levels of society. The creator of this 'high police' was Richelieu, who instituted a *cabinet noir* for methodically intercepting letters, and after him the lieutenant generals of police in Paris developed a systematic spy network designed to keep the government in touch with all sectors of society. As with Richelieu, his successors feared the political machinations of those in high places more than the revolutionary instincts of the Paris mob.

Another important feature of the police in pre-revolutionary France was its paternalism. A good deal of the secret police work under the *ancien régime* was designed to suppress private disorder and to avoid scandal in the best families and the court. Fontenelle wrote that it was essential for the police 'to penetrate into households by underground passages, and to keep on their behalf secrets which they had not confided for so long as it is not necessary to use them; to be present everywhere without being seen'.[7] People were secretly detained without trial in the interests of their families, either to avoid the scandal of a trial or because there were no grounds for a successful prosecution in the normal courts. Many of those held prisoner on the warrant of a *lettre de cachet* were ostensibly political prisoners in that their activities might be harmful to people in high places. The protective power of the police extended to protecting those private interests which the law could not properly care for, and which involved people whose reputation reflected on that of the court, the government or prominent families.

This mixture of intelligence work and paternalism formed the basis of Fouché's views on the proper role of the police. It is significant that his principal complaint against the police before the Revolution was that 'the Crown succumbed in 1789 because of the inefficiency of the police, those in office being incapable of unmasking the plots which threatened the royal house'.[8] (Other observers might reasonably have concluded that their main fault lay in not maintaining control of the streets of Paris.) It indeed seems clear that there was at this time a general view that the greatest police effort should be in the realm of politics, and that the best brains of the police service should be concerned with political matters rather than with the day-to-day ordering of public affairs. When after the Revolution, the Conseil des Cinq Cents (1795-99) decided that it was necessary to create a Ministry of Police to protect the republic, the rapporteur advanced the argument that it was necessary to have a police force guided by a minister 'with austere and firmly rooted republican principles who had not been changeable during the Revolution, and who had never deviated from the true line'. The impeccable nature of the credentials demanded was vital since the purpose of the force so created was to ensure that 'everything can be known, foreseen, and forestalled; carefully placed in public places, it must be able to recognise agitators, and take by surprise any treason which is being prepared'.[9]

With all this Fouché was in entire agreement. 'I felt,' he wrote, 'that all the daring, the skill of a statesmanlike minister should be absorbed in the "high police", and that what was left could safely be handed to heads of departments.' The minister of police, as he saw himself, should have 'the double mission of uncovering and dissolving coalitions and legal opposition to the established authority as well as the murky plots of royalists and foreign agents'. The minister alone should be the judge of internal politics, and observers and secret agents should only be considered important as his instruments. The 'high police' were not a matter of textbooks and reports, and 'the Minister himself should make contact with outstanding or influential men of every shade of opinion and doctrine in all the upper classes of the Nation'. This system, Fouché wrote later, always brought him success. 'I learnt more about the secret France from spoken and confidential communications and free conversations than from the hotch potch of reports that came to me.'[10]

The 'high police' then came to lie at the heart of the imperial police system. In Paris, despite the substantial administrative reforms of the police services, Fouché restricted his prefect of police (the descendant of the lieutenant general of police of the *ancien régime*) who should have been the great police administrator of Paris, to 'les filles, les boues, et les réverbères'. Elsewhere, as Fouché explained in 1805, the police, by which he meant the 'high police', were 'the regulating power which is felt everywhere, without ever being seen, and which, at the centre of the State, holds the place which the power which sustains the harmony of the celestial bodies holds in the universe, a power whose regularity strikes us although we are unable to divine the cause . . . Every branch of the administration has a part which subordinates it to the police.'[11]

Fouché also continued the paternalistic tradition of the old police. People continued to be detained secretly without trial in order to avoid public scandal, or because their activities or their reputation might be harmful to the good name of the state or prominent persons. Paternalism worked best without too much publicity, and discussion in the press or in salons could be prejudicial to the benevolent actions of the police. The police, thought Fouché, could substitute themselves should the law prove to be too blunt, or inadequate to deal equitably with a delicate situation. Being above the political and social battle, but conscious of it, the police had a flexibility denied to the politician, the judge or the journalist.

Fouché combined these two elements of high political sensitivity and paternalism in his own policies. He subverted all opposition to the regime without discrimination. He closed the Jacobin clubs in Paris, but he also infiltrated the right-wing Chouan resistance in the west of France. He was as concerned with neutralizing legal opposition to the regime as he was with disarming revolutionary plots. He regarded himself as a pacifier and was on excellent terms with both aristocrats and republicans. He acquired much information, as he pointed out, from his wide circle of acquaintances, but he mixed freely, not least in order to show the opponents of the regime the advantages of collaboration and compromise, and the disadvantages of resistance and rebellion. His aim was to have the regime accepted, and he tried to use the knowledge he obtained from the 'high police' to show that reconciliation could ensure peace and prosperity.

Fouché applied his own conception of the police to himself. He was the arbiter of society as well as its protector. Public order in itself was a moral good. The police by virtue of their special position were better placed to understand, and to help society to understand, the virtues of tranquillity, discipline and compromise. A French writer puts the argument very well:

> Even without written instructions the police knew instinctively how to recognise crimes and offences. The police knew too that they alone could judge correctly of the action to be taken against delinquents, because they had a general moral sense—a sense with which all mankind had been naturally endowed—and nature spoke so strongly in them that they admitted only with difficulty that a man who disagreed with them on some point or other could be honest and sincere. And they were alone in allying this moral certitude with a profound knowledge of the needs of public order.[12]

Throughout the nineteenth century this view of the moral, and indeed, artistic role of the police in society had an important influence on novelists and romancers, and we will return to it when we consider the nature of police psychology. Meanwhile, at this stage, it is worth summarizing the essential features of the traditional police state as it developed in Europe during the eighteenth and early nineteenth century. Its origins sprang from a desire to reform and modernize, and in order to achieve these aims its founders imposed a structured model of society and a formalized hierarchy of administration. The traditional police state was based on a rational division of labour within society and within administration, and its bureaucratic values of order, form and discipline extended from the offices to the citizen in his private as well as his public life. The necessity for order was rarely in dispute, and its imposition took two forms. First, the implementation of the police powers was itself a logical exercise which could be inferred by reference to the needs of the state, and which were then logically as well as politically correct. Second, it was accepted that order, decency and integrity did not come naturally to people, and human frailty could affect even administrators. Thus, only by a constant watch over all levels of society could the government become informed of the weak points in the organization of society and strengthen them. Only those who combined a profound knowledge of human weakness with a dispassionate concern for order could mount such a guard upon society itself. And these men, the police, were not simply the custodians of society, they were also its moral guardians and political censors.

3/The Police State in Transition

We have now distinguished three fundamental characteristics of the traditional police state. First, the paternal, benevolent, improving and devoted bureaucracy of Frederick II, rationally organized, exercising the police powers of the state on behalf of the sovereign. Second, the ubiquitous, silent secret police of Joseph II, organized as a parallel system of government, alert alike to the machinations of those in high places and to the conspiracies of the masses. Third, the elevation of the police as a state apparat by Fouché into the protector, censor and moral guide of society. Between 1815 and 1914 much of the institutional structure of European governments changed and new concepts of the state were developed, but these three characteristics not only profoundly affected the development of law and jurisprudence, but also the nature of public attitudes and social expectations.

To understand what happened we must revert to one simple idea. The 'police' meant the control of all internal administration which was not the concern of special functional institutions.[1] Between 1815 and 1870 the principal institutional change was the gradual dispersal of this control from a single ministry to other ministries and other bodies. In 1815 the Prussian minister of the interior had within his competence everything which referred to the basic constitution of the state and internal public law, and he controlled the entire internal state administration, including the police forces, with the exception of purely financial, military and judicial matters. In France, Fouché's special Ministry of Police was amalgamated with the Ministry of the Interior, so that this ministry too had over-all competence in internal affairs, including police administration. Since these ministries had a monopoly of national police powers and were the sole source of authority in internal administrative matters, they had subordinate bureaux and divisions concerned with public health, public works, transport, education and, in some cases, religious affairs. The growth of the work and specialization of these divisions during the first half of the century led to their acquiring an increasing degree of autonomy in their work. This autonomy eventually came to be recognized by their complete detachment from ministries of the interior to become ministries in their own right. They were still, however, regarded as technical ministries, and although they came to acquire regulatory powers in their special fields, the enforcement of these regulations remained very clearly a matter for the police authority under the control of the Ministry of the Interior. In the provinces the ordinance making power still formally rested with the Ministry of the Interior's officials. In general, then, it can be said that there was some dispersion of police powers, and ministries of the interior lost their welfare and technical functions to become more concerned with the general aspects of public security, health and morality, and with the organization and control of the country's police forces.

The second major institutional change was the gradual strengthening of the systems of local government. In France, Prussia and Austria, there was a gradual increase in the role allocated to elected elements, and an increasing degree of autonomy in purely local affairs. But this gradual relaxation of control did not extend to any wide dispersal of the police powers as such. A strong institutional infrastructure still remained. At each level of government responsibility was divided between local, elected representatives and officials appointed by the central government, what was known in Austria after the Stadion reforms as 'double track' administration: the lower the level of government, the greater the autonomy of the elected representatives. The chain of state control remained strong. In Prussia the *Landrat* was responsible for supervising the local authorities and for carrying out delegated state functions in his district. Above him, the *Regierungspraesident* of the region controlled and supervised the work of the *Landraete* and the mayors of big cities, and co-ordinated the work of the specialized central government officials in the field. And in the province the *Oberpraesident* presided over all the administrative services in the area, and represented the government and the crown.[2]

Similarly, in France, the prefect in the department, the sub-prefect in the arrondissement, and the mayor in the commune provided an authoritative chain of command which referred directly back to the Ministry of the Interior in Paris. The implementation of police powers, still regarded as the exclusive prerogative of the state, remained firmly under the central tutelage of the Ministry of the Interior, with the prefect acting as controlling agent in the field. As the police authorities, the prefect in the department and the mayor in the commune had a special concern with maintaining public order, security and health, and for these purposes had a special authority to make ordinances. In addition to these local police powers they had authority over the police forces in their area. These forces were organized on a national basis, again stretching back by way of the prefects to the Ministry of the Interior. The key professional police officer was the *commissaire de police*, who was responsible for maintaining the peace and also for detecting crime and apprehending offenders. The commissaire was assisted by uniformed men and in some of the larger cities by municipally recruited officers. He could call upon the national Gendarmerie for assistance, and that corps, although a military police force responsible to the minister of war, came operationally under the Ministry of the Interior when policing the countryside and small towns.

The political police remained an important element in government not only in France, but also in Germany and Austria throughout the nineteenth century. This was Metternich's Europe. As society became more complex, and waves of opposition to the state became an established feature of politics, no government felt that it could disarm itself by dismantling the political police service. The political police kept a special watch on the press, private associations and suspected revolutionaries. It was responsible for the surveillance of foreigners and political refugees. In many regimes it had authority to call for reports from other branches of the administration, and such reporting was often regarded as part of normal official duties. The overriding mission of the political police was to be constantly in a position to warn the government of the day of activities which were prejudicial to the safety of the state. Inevitably it collected information which was politically useful to the government or to individual ministers or officials, and its directors became powerful if shadowy figures.[3] The main efforts were concentrated in the capital cities, but important manufacturing centres also became places of interest.

The apparent ubiquity of the political police was part of its strength, but such evidence as there is suggests that popular rumour and imagination were very wide of the mark. The staff of the political police was frequently minimal, and its agents part time informants, working dubiously for payment by results. The use of provocateurs was also less usual than popularly supposed, and in France only the Paris police seem to have made widespread use of the practice.[4]

What was important in this context was that the primacy Fouché had given to the political police faded away. It was an essential element of government but it ceased to dominate the normal practices and routine of the official police forces. The evidence suggests that although the police services were ruthless enough in quelling disorders and harassing the opposition, the uniformed services in France, Germany and Austria as a whole developed an independent sense of professional integrity. They began to be a recognizable state apparat in their own right. Even under the Austrian government or under the Second Empire in France, charges of wanton brutality or the excessive use of force were significantly rare. Critics of the police were

still more concerned with accusing the police of political moti-
vation rather than of violence. In France, at least, there is
also evidence that charges against the police were properly in-
vestigated, and offenders punished. The professional journal of
the commissaires de police constantly stressed the high nature of
the police mission, and the need to use police powers with common sense and integrity.[5] There was never any doubt, however,
that the control of police forces, as well as the exercise of police
powers, was a matter of central concern to the state, and that
European governments intended to retain that monopoly.

The third institutional development was the result of the
growth of social and welfare legislation. The police authorities
in the traditional police state had not only repressive but also
protective and welfare functions. The Prussian distinction was
between the *Sicherheitspolizei*, which was to preserve the individual from dangers threatening his person or his property, and
the *Wohlfahrtspolizei* which was to further the public welfare by
the promotion of interests beneficial to society. Whereas in
Britain police legislation at this time was entirely concerned
with the maintenance of order and the repression of crime,
European countries considered police activity to be not only
concerned with prohibiting activities prejudicial to public welfare, but also with prescribing the performance of certain positive acts which were either held to be beneficial to society as a
whole or would make recourse to repression unnecessary. Therefore, as new legislation designed to meet new social needs was
passed, laying positive duties on individuals, corporations or
companies, the enforcement and supervision of the new laws
remained the responsibility of the traditional police authorities.
They did not become, as in the common law countries, the
responsibility of newly created national, municipal or *ad hoc*
departments.

This development meant that the police authorities on the
Continent were given statutory powers to promulgate rules and
ordinances regulating the conduct of citizens in respect of all

the functions coming within both their old and their new jurisdiction. The police authorities were, consequently, the principal
beneficiaries of the new and extensive power of delegated legislation. In Prussia, the law of March 11, 1850 gave to police
authorities the power to issue ordinances relating to the protection of persons and property, traffic and markets, public
meetings, the surveillance of foreigners, and many other matters;
it included, moreover, a blanket authority to make regulations
and ordinances for 'all else which must be regulated through the
police power in the interest of the communes and their members'.
This law was the basis of hundreds of police ordinances touching
every conceivable human activity. It gave the police authority
powers not only to protect society as a whole, but also to prescribe individual conduct; 'thus a house owner must sprinkle his
street in hot weather when ordered by the police, or a certain
striker must refrain from picketing when so directed, or a given
contractor must remove building encumbrances on demand'.[6]

This power to make ordinances was subject only to the supervision of the superior administrative authorities, who, at their
discretion, could annul or amend police regulations. With the
ordinance making police power went judicial authority to inflict
summary punishments without recourse to the courts. Furthermore, officials of all kinds, and in particular officials exercising
the police powers of the state, were immune to legal proceedings
brought against them by injured parties if they could show that
they were acting in the course of their official duties. Proceedings against an official could only effectively be initiated by the
minister or superior administrative authority. It was virtually
impossible to bring actions for false imprisonment or illegal
arrest against even individual police officers. Redress remained
a matter of bureaucratic rather than judicial sanctions.

Meanwhile, however, the whole question of the police power
was being increasingly analysed and rationalized, in particular by
French jurists. The argument went like this. The police function
was fundamental to the sovereign power, but certain important

distinctions could be made. The police power involved two different functions. The first was the administrative police function which had as its purpose the maintenance of public order, public morality and public welfare. This inevitably implied that the police authority should have its own ordinance making power in order to prescribe the limits of permissible conduct in these fields, and to take any necessary measures in advance to protect society. In its turn the administrative police power could be divided into two parts, a general, national police power (the *police générale*), and a local municipal police power (the *police municipale*). The general police power was vested in the head of the state, the minister and a small number of designated officials. This police power was the executive arm of the legislative authorities, and it was responsible for implementing and, if necessary, supplementing the general rules of law governing society. In a constitutional state, the exercise of these powers would always be subject in the last resort to the highest political authority in the country, the representatives of the nation. Similarly, although an independent field of operation could be accepted for those responsible for the general police, in that the highest police authority had a special independent responsibility for protecting the state from threats to its integrity or continuity, a political sanction would always remain, even where there was no judical redress.

At the lower levels the local, municipal police were concerned with the proper administration of the public services intimately affecting the domestic interests of citizens, public peace, sanitation, weights and measures, markets, highways and traffic. The mayors of the communes, subject to the tutelage of the prefects and sub-prefects, acted as the police authority in these matters, having an ordinance making power in their own right which they drew from the state. They could call upon the police services in their commune to enforce these ordinances, and the local commissaire de police and the local Gendarmerie were required to give them all necessary assistance. That is, at all levels the exercise of police powers, and the control of police forces were vested in the same office: at the national level, the minister of the interior, at the departmental level, the prefects, at the commune level, the mayors, each level being subject to the supervision of the superior, the minister having an ultimate responsibility to the highest political organ of the state.

The administrative police function was contrasted with the judicial or repressive police function, the *police judiciaire*. The key to this system was the commissaire de police. As we have seen, he was required to use his police resources if necessary to enforce the regulations and ordinances promulgated by the police authorities. He was also responsible for the detection of crime and the apprehension of offenders. When he acted as an officer of the police judiciare, however, the commissaire de police came under the control of the judicial and not the administrative authorities. He then acted under the instructions of the *juges d'instruction* and the *procureurs de la République*, officials of the Ministry of Justice who were members of the national corps of magistrates. These officers had the judicial responsibility for determining whether to bring charges against offenders and whether to prosecute them, and they carried out the initial judicial enquiry. Offenders were sent forward to trial on their writ, and they acted as prosecuting attorneys in the courts.

This corps of magistrates developed into a healthy check on the operations of the police authorities. The magistrates were for the most part very conservative lawyers, very conscious of their independence from the normal administration, and aware of their ultimate responsibility for the proper administration of justice. As with all other jurists, they recognized the right of the state to use exceptional powers in emergencies, but even during the Second Empire, when France reverted to the more traditional forms of the police state, the procureurs de la République resisted all attempts by the prefects to base their administrative authority on such an arbitrary source as the general police power, which they rightly regarded as virtually uncontrollable by normal judicial procedures. Their resistance was especially effective when, in classic style, a special Ministry of Police was to be created. Their pressure led to the introduction of far more substantial legal safeguards in the text, and their consistent hostility to the ministry's pretensions had a good deal to do with the new ministry's rapid demise. To this extent, the efforts of French jurists to bring analysis and rationality to administrative law had become an accepted part of educated thinking, and it had important political results.

The major political preoccupation of European jurists after 1870 was how to tame the sovereign powers of the state on which the traditional police state had been based. A good deal had been done in constitutional terms to break down the authoritarian basis of government, but in two important respects the police powers of the state still managed to escape political and judicial control.

French and German jurists now began to diverge in their views.[7] Until the middle 1860s German jurists continued to teach the doctrine of the patrimonial state in which public power was the personal right of the prince. In 1865 Gerber propounded an ostensibly new doctrine which, in fact, harked back to early Roman law. He held that the state was itself a juridical person distinct from the person of the prince; the prince and the nation were simply organs of the state. This transcendental view of the state came to be widely accepted by German jurists, and even by the turn of the century, the great jurist Jellinek still argued that 'sovereignty means to command unconditionally, and to be able to exercise irresistible force; it is the public power, a power of will which is never determined except by itself; that is precisely sovereignty'. This meant in theory that there was no legal relationship between the organs of state and the state itself, any more than there is between an individual and his several senses. It meant, in practice, that the state was justified in acting not solely in the interests of its citizens, but in the interests of the state as a whole, and the executive was in a better position to determine what these ends were than was any other organ of state. Public administration, therefore, did not exist simply to provide welfare and protective services to the public, but to serve the ends of the almost metaphysically defined state itself.

French jurists proposed a fundamentally different doctrine. They argued, first, that the sovereign was the nation, and not the state, least of all some mystical entity which could only be defined in a circular way. The sovereign nation delegated its powers to its representatives, the governors of the country. The inevitable corollary to this argument was that the representatives of the nation, the politicians, acquired a primacy over the administration and the executive totally unknown in Germany or Austria-Hungary.

Indeed, French jurists began to go further and to question the whole notion of sovereignty itself. Hauriou denied that sovereign power was the essence of public law. There would always, admittedly, be a power to dominate, but it was no longer a subjective right possessed by the state; it was above all a social function. Berthelémy pushed this argument further still: 'Acts of authority performed by the administration do not involve the notion of a juridical person in whose name they are performed. ... It is a great mistake to regard the use of power as an exercise of rights. The officials who command do not exercise the rights of a sovereign; they perform functions, the totality of which, if you will, constitutes the sovereign power.'[8]

France was by now moving decisively away from traditional jurisprudence. Not only was the theory of a patrimonial estate being rejected, but the very basis of sovereignty was under attack. This rejection of past theories was of fundamental importance in bringing the police authorities under political control. The question was now posed as to whether judicial control could also be extended over public administration.

The traditional view of administrative responsibility was that

the official was subordinate to his superior, and the superior in
the last resort to the highest state authority. We have seen how
the Cameralists justified this view in the traditional police state.
By a historical quirk, the Cameralists' view of the immunity of
the executive from judicial control was supported by liberal
theorists, supporters of Montesquieu. For them the doctrine of
the separation of powers involved the executive being independent of the judiciary in the same way as the judiciary was
independent of the legislature. This doctrine was strengthened
by memories of conservative provincial parlements under
the *ancien régime* resisting all efforts of the central government
to bring about much-needed structural reforms. From the
earliest days of the French Revolution the doctrine of executive
independence was enshrined in constitutional law. The law of
16–24 August 1790, was explicit: 'the judicial function is distinct
and will always remain separate from the administrative function. Judges will not, on pain of dismissal, interfere in any way
whatsoever with the operation of the administration, nor will
they call before them administrative officials for matters arising
out of their official functions.' As a result of this measure, not
only were officials responsible solely to their administrative
superiors, but they were also given immunity from prosecution
for any act they performed in an official capacity.

Napoleon created the *Conseil d'État* to advise him on administrative matters, and to a certain extent it had some judicial
control of the administrative services. But after Napoleon's
downfall, the Conseil d'État was regarded as the creation and
tool of an authoritarian regime, and was the object of much
suspicion by liberal reformers. The result was to leave public
administration, including the police authorities, free of all
judicial control, except where a plain violation of law was concerned. The minister was the ultimate judge of administrative
procedure and of the equity and necessity of administrative acts.
After 1870 a determined effort was made to change this
situation.[9]

The theory of administrative immunity from judicial procedures was challenged even within the context of traditional notions about sovereignty held by German jurists. They proferred alternative explanations of the role the judiciary should play in the state. The first they called the *Justizstaat* in which conflicts between public authorities and ordinary citizens would be dealt with by the ordinary courts of the land. This was still consonant with the idea of sovereign powers, the state simply recognizing that in many cases public authorities were acting as normal contracting parties and could safely accept the jurisdiction of the courts. The weakness of this doctrine, however, was that the courts could only deal with matters involving contract or breaches of the law; they could not intervene where the exercise of administrative discretion affected citizens' rights where no laws had been broken. Furthermore, it was in precisely those fields which jurists recognized as still being within the state's autonomous authority that conflicts of equity, necessity and abuse of power were most likely to arise.

The alternative to the Justizstaat was the *Rechtsstaat*. Its supporters, among whom Gneist was the acknowledged leader, held that the actions of the state and its agents were based upon public law, and that this was a distinctive branch of law to some extent separable from constitutional law. What was needed, therefore, was a specialized administrative jurisdiction developing its own law and precedents. The Rechtsstaat was one in which a judicial body, independent of the executive but attached to it, would keep constantly under review the administrative acts of the state and the state authorities. It would have powers to annul acts which were corrupt in form or intent, or involved illegal or perverted use of administrative discretion or the police power.

In 1872 the French Conseil d'État was reorganized and given statutory competence to deal with all matters of administrative litigation as well as to deal directly with appeals against administrative acts of state officials. The new German empire gradually followed suit, and new administrative jurisdictions were created, the most important being introduced in Prussia in 1883. No imperial jurisdiction was ever created since it was held that this would intrude on the autonomy of the several states. One significant difference between the German and French administrative jurisdictions was that the French Conseil d'État had jurisdiction in all litigation involving public authorities and private citizens, unless a law specifically provided otherwise. In Germany and Austria the opposite was true: a court's jurisdiction was limited to matters specified in the law, and all other matters either went to another court or were subject to no legal redress at all.

Thus, we can see that by the end of the nineteenth century the institutional and theoretical bases of the traditional police state had been demolished. The notion of sovereignty itself was under attack; the concept of the police power as an amorphous and all-pervasive basis of government had been refined and rationalized and brought under intellectual control; and the activities of the police authorities had been brought within the orbit of judicial control.

Remnants of the old traditions continued, however, to exist. The Conseil d'État accepted that there were acts of government which, involving the highest political discretion, must remain completely outside the control of the courts. It also accepted that a distinction must still be made between those acts of public power, for which there could be no legal redress except by grace, and those acts of normal administration, which could be dealt with by the administrative courts.

But in France this continuity of authoritarian jurisprudence had to be set against the change of tone in administrative and political life after 1875. The ethos of administration altered, and a sense of responsibility to the republic rather than to the prince or to some transcendental state helped to throw off the psychological shackles of the past. The dependence of ministers on the Chamber of Deputies, of prefects on political ministers of the interior, of mayors on local electorates, led to a more careful and responsive use of the police powers. There was a greater belief in the virtues of reason, and a relative decline in the traditional authoritarian pattern of administrative attitudes. The need for strong central control of the police was almost universally accepted as the basis for government, but this control was itself continually under public scrutiny, not only by parliament but by administrative courts and a critical electorate.

Public attitudes and social expectations seem, however, not to have changed as significantly in Germany and Austria. The attacks on the theoretical basis of the traditional police state had been less energetic and fundamental than in France, even though there had been many comparable institutional and judicial changes. The general tendency even of reforming jurists was to concentrate upon disciplining the exercise of state powers in order to protect individual rights, assuming that concern for individual freedom was unnecessary as it would follow automatically from the control of the arbitrary use of state powers.

The best evidence suggests that this was too sanguine a view. In the years before the First World War an American, R. Fosdick, made a comparative study of European police systems, and his observations confirm the continuity of administrative attitudes and public expectations. Fosdick accepted the differences of political and social philosophy which distinguished the mores of German populations from those of the societies he was accustomed to in Britain and the United States. These populations were inclined to favour a paternal and regulatory system of government. Fosdick also accepted the special police problems that countries such as Austria had to face with multi-national rivalries. They lent force to the argument for strong centralized police forces. The senior police authorities themselves were strikingly competent, educated and dedicated officials. The closeness of police supervision over the population was held by those concerned to be 'simply indicative of the solicitude of the state for its own; it is a systematic, domestic arrangement, representing internal order and discipline'.[10] Other observers also frequently commented upon the orderly, structured and largely contented populations of the German states at this time, and recognized the dedication and sense of purpose of the officials who in many cases had made their countries pioneers of social legislation.

Fosdick, however, was also concerned with the other side of the coin. He found many examples of continuing authoritarianism and the arbitrary use of police powers both in the German states and in Austria-Hungary. The ordinance making power was used by the police authorities to regulate minute details of public conduct, and their judicial powers of summary conviction were sometimes openly abused. Police officers were protected from 'insult', and their superiors accepted no challenge to their sworn evidence. The fundamental rights of citizens and the effectiveness of court decisions were paralysed by police authorities 'whenever in their judgement, matters arise involving a danger to public security and quiet'.[11] Suspects, for instance, who could legally only be held for twenty-four hours before being brought before a magistrate, were detained for weeks simply by the police authorities charging them seriatim with breaches of one of the innumerable police ordinances. In Austria, the arbitrariness of the police was reinforced by the many enactments which hedged the liberties of the citizen, and which included a rigorous press censorship and stiff public assembly laws.

Fosdick was also critical of police methods. In his view the ordinary police officers lacked initiative, imagination and adaptability, and this was largely due to the system. The methods of investigation were largely inquisitorial in nature, and physical pressure was not uncommon. In the event of a crime the police would systematically interrogate everyone in the vicinity whether or not there was any evidence against them. Crimes were solved by a process of elimination, each witness having to prove his innocence to the satisfaction of the police.

German police authorities had a complex and detailed method of registering all persons in their area, the *Meldwesen*, whereby all inhabitants, of whatever nationality, had to report their comings and goings to the local police authorities, who then elaborately cross-checked and indexed all arrivals and departures. This allowed the police to track suspects, or check alibis with the minimum of trouble.

The Berlin police, in particular, relied to a considerable extent upon voluntary informers, who had no official standing and could not make arrests. They received three marks a day and their expenses, and were widely used to keep an eye on social matters as well as criminal activities. An unknown number of spies were directly employed by the police to infiltrate political movements and to discover their policies and intentions. Fosdick's estimate was that about one hundred spies and informers were involved.

Fosdick also cast some doubt upon the generally complacent view of the role of the police in society. Most subordinate police officers in Austria and the German states were recruited directly from the army, and this led to behaviour whose arrogance would not be tolerated in a democratic society. A Berlin *Schutzmann's* normal behaviour on duty 'would provoke a riot in two hours in Trafalgar Square'.[12] In Fosdick's view the police forces in Germany and Austria were the right arm of the ruling classes, responsible to the crown or the higher authorities, and not to the people. The arbitrariness of the police in the exercise of their duties 'has bred a lively animosity particularly among the poorer classes. . . . To a large extent this is due to the fact that the police represent the imperial government, and thus the domination of the bureaucracy.'[13] The police had come to typify the arbitrary use of bureaucratic power, and popular feeling ran against the political use of the police rather than against central control as such.

It will be seen, therefore, that despite the institutional and theoretical changes which had taken place in Europe during the nineteenth century, it was still possible in 1914 to trace back important social, political, and administrative elements to the traditional police state: the dominant, paternalistic bureaucracy of Frederick II, the surveillance of society by the secret police of Joseph II, and the role of the police apparat as the arbiter, censor and moral guide of society, as first elaborated by the great master, Fouché.

4/New Meanings of the Term

The common law countries stood outside of this process, and, indeed, they regarded the whole matter of 'the police' with the utmost suspicion. Radzinowicz has shown that the word itself entered the English language in the eighteenth century and it was for some time used in the wide European sense. Swift used it in this way, and Johnson defined it in his *Dictionary* as 'the regulation and government of a city or country, so far as regards the inhabitants'. Burke used it in the sense of 'policy', and Pitt described emergency war legislation as a measure of 'war police'. In Scotland, always more open to European influence, both senses of the word were employed as 'a public police', and Adam Smith defined it as 'the second general division of jurisprudence ... which properly signified the policy of civil government', although he went on to add that 'it now only means the regulation of the inferior parts of government, viz. the cleanliness, security and cheapness of plenty'.[1]

During the long and animated discussion in the eighteenth century about the reform of internal order it was clear that it was precisely the European connotations of the word which most annoyed or alarmed the English, reminding them of the Star Chamber and the constitutional struggles of the previous century. Englishmen and foreigners alike agreed that they were prepared to endure an unusual degree of violence in the streets and a consequential lack of personal security rather than to risk the incursions on their personal liberty which they considered was the price Europeans had to pay for their 'police'. They preferred, said a French writer, 'to be robbed by wretches of desperate fortune than to be persecuted by the executive'. Much of the hostility to the reform of internal order arose from the use made

50

by its opponents of the tyrannical associations aroused by the word police. Reformers such as John Fielding and Colquhoun came therefore to restrict its meaning to that less damaging sense of 'such part of the social organisation as is concerned immediately with the maintenance of good order, or the prevention or detection of offences'. Gradually over the years it came to be limited to this sense, and was used as a synonym for the constabulary. In the nineteenth century it was virtually always used in this sense, and British jurists had better things to do than to engage too deeply in formal and theoretical discussions of 'the police power'.

It is, indeed, more common to find the term properly used in its widest sense across the North Atlantic where it had entered the language in the latter part of the eighteenth century. It can be found almost in the sense of 'national security' in 1812 in the Quebec announcement of the commencement of hostilities. Strikingly headed with the single word 'Police' it informed the population that 'Whereas authentic intelligence has been received that the Government of the United States of America did, on the 18th instant, declare War against the United Kingdom of Great Britain and Ireland and its dependencies, Notice is hereby given that all Subjects and Citizens of the said United States, and all persons claiming Citizenship, are ordered to quit the City of Quebec . . . on pain of arrest.' The same notice ordered the constables of the city of Quebec to assemble in the police office on the following day, thus making it clear that the two senses of the word 'police' were being used simultaneously at that time.[2]

American jurists have continued to use the concept of 'the police power' with far greater freedom than their English counterparts, and in its broadest, European, sense. From the literature it appears that American authorities accept that 'the police power' undoubtedly covers the protection of the health, safety and morals of the community. From it stems the authority to regulate trade, sanitation, traffic, places of entertainment and public exhibitions. Its limits remain imprecise because of the changing nature of the jurisprudence of the Supreme Court; public attitudes have accepted wider definitions of the public interest as society has changed. It is the least defined of state powers, and its scope has been extended to authorize the conservation of natural resources, zoning legislation, the protection of the public against fraud and the enforced destruction of private property. The Supreme Court has always maintained its right to be the ultimate arbiter of the proper use of the police power, and for some time it held that it was a power reserved to the states, and that the federal government had no such inherent power. But this view has also been reversed, and the court now apparently looks at the degree of arbitrariness involved in the proposed legislation.

But despite this acceptance of the theoretical notion of 'the police' Americans have shared with the English an extreme suspicion of policemen and police services, and in both countries their efficiency has always been subordinated to their political dependence. Only with the greatest reluctance has any form of centralization been accepted, and although under pressure of social upheavals both countries created a branch of police with particular concern for political activities (the British Special Branch to deal with the Irish troubles, the Federal Bureau of Investigation, originally called Bureau of Investigation and set up in 1908 to deal with labour troubles) in neither country have these services a uniformed sister-service of national competence from whom they can demand assistance *manu militari* as of right. And common law jurists have never used the term 'police state' in a neutral technical sense, useful in comparative jurisprudence, as European jurists have done and, in some of the literature, still do.

On the rare occasions in the nineteenth century when English-speaking writers used the term 'police state' there was an undoubted note of moral condemnation. *The Times* of

September 6, 1865, noted, for instance, that 'Austria was long known on the Continent as "the police state", and M. von Weiss will again obtain for her that unenviable title'. The translation of 'Polizeistaat' into 'police state' however seems not to have taken place until the 1930s. The files of the *Oxford English Dictionary* suggest that the translation with its modern pejorative connotations came about with reference to the National Socialist state in Germany after 1933. It seems to have entered the language through journalists rather than through constitutional lawyers or political scientists. The *New Statesman* of January 15, 1938, has: 'Meanwhile, the atmosphere of "the police state" is already with us.' In 1939, the *War Illustrated* had the highly significant sentence: 'Spies are everywhere; indeed, Germany is the modern exemplification of "the police state" in action.' Finally, Webster's *Third International Dictionary* came to define it as 'a political unit (as a nation) characterised by repressive governmental control of political, economic and social life usually by an arbitrary exercise of power by the police, and especially the secret police, in place of the regular operation of the administrative and judicial organs of government according to established legal processes'.

If this last definition refers to the Polizeistaat in its traditional form it is plainly inaccurate. Enlightened citizens no doubt found the state's omnipresence somewhat claustrophobic and stifling, but as we have seen in three examples no one expected the state to use repression as an end in itself. The state's ends were entirely laudable by modern standards (though less so for nineteenth-century liberals and radicals) since the intention of the governors of the Polizeistaat was to create orderly and predictable government for economic growth and social welfare.

Nor was the bureaucracy in the Polizeistaat expected to act in an arbitrary way. As we have seen, the bureaucracy was bound by a complex system of laws and regulations, and secretly supervised to see that it performed its duties honestly, punctiliously and equitably. And although civil servants exercised the police power on behalf of the state it would be historically ridiculous to regard them as policemen. Even if, as Fouché wished, the impression was created that the police were everywhere, he clearly never made the claim that his men were running the administration, nor in a general sense that they had replaced the judiciary.

We have, therefore, that not unknown phenomenon in political science of a term being changed from its original technical meaning into a term of abuse or praise. The original sense becomes lost as the term is degraded into common usage, and ceases to have technical validity. Very few people who indiscriminately use the term 'Fascist', for instance, can explain its proper sense.

Probably what happened was this. The Weimar Republic which came into being after the First World War prided itself on having transformed Germany into a Rechtsstaat. It had all the appurtenances of such a state, which its jurists regarded as being the most advanced and civilized form of society. When it collapsed after the 1933 elections to be replaced by the National Socialist regime of Hitler, Germany became—technically for European jurists—a Polizeistaat once again. This by a simple process of elimination. It had ceased to be a Rechsstaat; it clearly was not a Justizstaat; it had many of the characteristics of the traditional Polizeistaat.

There was nothing particularly perverse in this line of reasoning, nor was it excessively pedantic. If it were possible to elucidate a juridical theory underlying Hitler's political utterances, it could be summarized as a demand for a state capable of looking after itself in foreign affairs, based on a society which was strong, cohesive and disciplined. Political dissent, which threatened the stability of the state was not to be permitted, and the state was to be subordinated to a single political directing will, utilizing a strong administrative state hierarchy of officials, with the explicit aims of centralizing the national effort, mobilizing society and creating national self-consciousness. Its economic doctrine owed more to the mercantilists than to Marshall, and had a most explicit welfare function built into it. In so far as jurists would view it, the National Socialist state would fall squarely into the definition of the Polizeistaat used in the *German Encyclopedia*:

> A state which emphasizes welfare and law and order in the widest sense of the word. It assumed the right to un-restricted interference in the private affairs of its subjects, especially with their property and liberty in order to expand the general welfare and for the protection of public security and order. Owing to its close control of culture and the economy and the restrictions it placed on individual liberty, it was vehemently attacked by the emerging liberal bourgeois movement.

If jurists saw the National Socialist state in this way, other foreign observers became more obsessed with the political reality rather than with the juridical theory. The elimination of dissent was by murder, tyranny and the concentration camp. The subordination of the state to a single directing political will involved the strutting of evil men on the public stage, and the ravings of the apparently demented. The strength of the self-disciplined nation appeared to have as its principal purpose the destruction of innocent minorities and the deliberate incitement to unprovoked aggression. Welfare economics was the basis for the war machine, and mobilization had war, not development, as its declared purpose.

The disciplined, responsive and responsible bureaucracy appeared to have been freed from the psychological and bureaucratic limitations imposed by a doctrine of paternal government. The citizen was subordinated to the machine, the machine to the party, the party to the Führer, the Führer to his demon. Whereas Frederick II could call himself the first servant of the state, and mean it, under the National Socialist regime the citizen became the last servant of the party.

And, to the outside world, the party in turn came to be symbolized by the apparently ubiquitous party, political and secret police, and few observers cared to distinguish between the party, the *Sicherheitsdienst*, the *Geheimestaatspolizei* and the *Schutzstaffel*. The regime seemed to have as its base a fanfaronade of parading, vicious and paranoiac bullies deliberately creating, and then enjoying, an atmosphere of terror. Tales of secret horror, the sudden and permanent disappearance of innocent people, the very attack on the concept of innocence itself, and the apparent devotion of a nation's police services to endless and mindless sadism became commonplace.

To the informed observer the National Socialist state seemed to be an amalgam of the formal administrative structure and traditions of the traditional Polizeistaat with a new and hideous ideology. The new version seemed to be dedicated to unreason, passion and hysteria, a long way from the atmosphere of the Enlightenment. Conscientious, industrious and methodical bureaucrats were regarded as having become the instruments of mad, evil and vicious men. It was like using a Rolls Royce not in order to carry passengers in comfort, but to run people down in the street.

This simple translation of 'Polizeistaat' into 'police state', bringing with it a whole baggage of emotions and prejudices, has had the effect of altering the technical sense of the term. 'Police state' has come to be used in reference to an amorphous category of states, whose principal, and perhaps only common characteristic is that they offend the instincts of liberals and men of good will. It has been used in this sense as a term of abuse for both Batista's and Castro's Cuba, Communist China, Formosa, Yugoslavia, South Africa, Portugal, most Latin American countries at one time or other, Spain, Indonesia, Czechoslovakia, Greece, Morocco, Saudi Arabia, Algeria—the list seems endless.

There is little point in dwelling on this evolution of political vocabulary any further: if we wish to keep the term 'police state' for technical purposes we will have to disregard its emotional overtones for the time being. We will turn, therefore, to an analysis of exactly what happened in National Socialist Germany in order to see what precise features of government gave that state a distinctive institutional framework different from that of other authoritarian regimes.

5/The Modern Police State

The administrative history of National Socialist Germany falls into two parts.* The first was from 1933 to 1939, the time when both German jurists, and, later, foreign observers recognized that Germany was a police state with definable characteristics. We shall call Germany in this period a 'modern police state'. Between 1939 and 1944 there were further major institutional developments which led to a qualitative change in the nature of the state. These later changes were not simply the usual administrative abnormalities which occur in time of war. They were the result of deliberate and sustained efforts to alter the internal balance of power within the state. The success of these efforts created a new form of state, which we will call the 'totalitarian police state'. The totalitarian police state was as different in kind from its predecessor, the modern police state, as the modern police state was from its predecessor, the traditional police state. It is important to distinguish these three categories analytically as a good deal of confusion has been caused by indiscriminately lumping them together in a single amorphous group.

We must isolate the principal institutional and juridical changes which occurred in Germany from 1933 to 1939 in order to present a formal account of the abstract features of the modern police state. To do this with the greatest clarity we will divide the following description into three parts: first, the con-

* A formal analysis, similar to the one in this chapter and in chapter 8, could be made of the development of the U.S.S.R. in the period 1919–39. But as the term 'police state' comes into English from the German, and because of the limitations of space, it seemed better to limit myself to a close study of the evolution of National Socialist Germany.

stitutional changes which were introduced; second, the development of the police administration; third, the effects of this development upon the other major state institutions.

The Weimar Republic was constitutionally a semi-federal parliamentary democracy, and, administratively, a Rechtsstaat. It combined all the recognized features of liberal democracy: universal suffrage, separation of powers, checks and balances, judicial control of the administration, organized political parties, a skeleton army, a free press, stalwart trade unions and liberty of conscience. The one feature that it grievously lacked as a model state was a monopoly of the means of coercion. The Weimar Republic relied for its authority on reason, enlightened self-interest, good intentions and social improvement. Its opponents relied upon passion, revenge, destruction, organized violence and hate. Its liberalism was a living offence to radicals of the left, its democracy to radicals of the right. It was harassed by its war-time conquerors, denigrated by its ex-servicemen, ruined by its economists, manipulated by its civil servants, subverted by its army and demoralized by its intellectuals. The tribulations of the Weimar Republic are a matter of history, and are now simply a good historical example of the pathology of liberalism and the inefficacy of piety in an immoral world.

The major constitutional changes which the National Socialist regime introduced after its accession to power in 1933 were the abolition of the main features of liberal democracy. Political parties were banned and the National Socialist movement given the monopoly of public political expression; parliament was deprived of its powers and reduced to a formal auditorium; the press was placed under close censorship; the semi-federal nature of government was replaced by an extreme form of political, and later administrative, centralization; trade unions were placed under official party control; the army was strengthened, universal conscription was introduced, and the educational system and youth movements used to foster civic virtues rather than cultural values. All these changes were classic steps in the creation of an authoritarian state, and they were justified on traditional grounds: improvement, protection, welfare, mobilization, modernization and development. The National Socialist philosophy had, of course, its own special definitions of these terms, as all ideologies have; in particular it included racial origins in its definition of political dissent, and the means by which political dissent was eliminated consequently finally included genocide.

The constitutional changes necessary to transform Germany from a liberal democracy into an authoritarian regime were in practice remarkably simple. First, Hitler turned the Weimar consitution against itself. As with most constitutions it contained provision for reserve powers. Article 48 gave the federal minister of the interior general responsibility for the over-all supervision of law and order in the country. This was used to instal Reich commissioners in all the *Länder* in which the National Socialist party had no legislative majority. This step effectively introduced political centralization.

Next, a permanent state of emergency was introduced which would provide a legal basis for any subsequent institutional or juridical changes. The Reichstag fire furnished the pretext for promulgating the famous 'Ordinance for the Protection of the People and the State' on February 28, 1933, and this became the effective constitutional basis for Hitler's future authority. This ordinance in effect introduced parallel systems of government. On the one hand it was used to create new institutions and to introduce new legal principles which drew their sole authority from the state of emergency. On the other hand, it allowed the normal state machinery of government to co-exist where it could serve a useful purpose. The ordinance 'specifically dispensed with the normal state system though theoretically leaving it in being'.[1] It enabled Hitler, as head of state, to by-pass the normal legal processes whenever he wished to do so while ostensibly remaining within the confines of the law. The party and the police were given certain official attributes of the state whenever it was formally necessary for them to have them. The creation and operation of concentration camps was based on this ordinance. It allowed the police to impinge on the police powers of the civil service without officially taking them over, and it circumvented judicial control of the activities of the political police without directly challenging the judiciary's authority. The passionate concern of German officials for order and form was turned against them. The ordinance was used to legalize activities, when the 'forms' required it, which would not have been countenanced by the judicial and administrative authorities acting on their own authority. It allowed Hitler, the party and the police to transform Germany into a state without an opposition while evading a head-on conflict with the established powers of the civil service, the army and the judiciary, until such time as they had built up their own strength.

The use of reserve constitutional powers and the introduction of a permanent state of emergency have become the common means for introducing authoritarian systems of government. Hitler, however, added a third constitutional innovation, one which can only be used by charismatic leaders. He invented an extra-constitutional source of power for himself. As in Augustan Rome, Hitler, as Führer, laid claim to an authority vested in him by sources other than the legitimate powers of his formal office as head of state. His supremacy over the state machinery of government was properly based on the constitutional doctrine of the ordering of office and the legality of succession. The established authorities of the state then had a duty to obey within the competence of their official positions. Hitler added to this the claim to a peculiar type of personal sanctity which stemmed from his supposedly unique position as the embodiment of the German people. This claim formed the basis of the party's ideology. But no conventional instrument of government in a civilized country could normally have accepted so extraordinary an assumption of extra-constitutional authority, with its accompanying claim to pre-emptive personal leadership, and the claim was therefore formulated in terms of a 'new philosophy'.

This 'new philosophy' simply stated that in the National Socialist theory of government no limits could be placed on the authority of the Führer as the embodiment of the people working through the party. The Führer was bound by neither positive nor moral law. His historic mission and the destiny of the German people overrode all considerations of legal formalism. Party jurists traced this claim back, on the one hand, to the metaphysical jurisprudence of earlier times—and, indeed, could quote such recent authors as Otto Mayer who, in the 1920s, still defined the police 'as that which gives the whole its distinctive mark, and becomes a comprehensive and systematic working-up of the human material available in order to lead it towards a greater goal'.[2] On the other hand, they could refer directly back to the harder traditions of the *raison d'état* of the traditional police state and the Cameralists. In this atmosphere it was easy to refer obscurely to the 'new philosophy' and claim, for instance, that 'the common law of the Reich recognises the authority of the political police', when patently no law did any such thing. It was simply an expression of the new philosophy drawing on mythical extra-constitutional powers.

In order to formalize this new philosophy and its expression through the party and the Führer, the party was given the status of a corporate body by the law of December 1, 1933. This law, the 'Guarantees for the Unity of the Party and the State', introduced the obscurity of the new philosophy into the law itself. On one view it fused the state and the party together; on another it simply recognized the party's claim to political leadership over the state.[3] Some party institutions were given state powers, but it has been well argued that it is false to regard the party as a state institution simply because certain of its subsidiary organizations were given official attributes. They could properly be regarded simply as a camouflage, giving an official appearance to non-official instructions from the Führer.[4] One simple proposition emerged from all this obscurity. The party represented the people, and the task of the state administration was to use its resources to achieve the aims set for it by the party. The party, however, had a single voice, and that was the voice of the Führer.

In this way, two parallel sources of law were introduced into German constitutional law: a state authority which was based upon traditional constitutional and administrative law and the state of emergency to provide the normal machinery of government; and an extra-constitutional authority, vested in the Führer, which knew no limitations except his will, which took precedence over the state's authority whenever the single directing will decreed that it was expedient. The state's authority, then, was simply used to give an official seal to the Führer's non-official decrees. The police as well as the party greatly benefited from such an extra-constitutional source of authority and we therefore must now consider the development of the police as a leading state apparat in Germany in the period up to 1939.

The Weimar Republic had introduced changes in the general structure of police administration as it existed before 1914.

In 1918, after the First World War, the new People's Commissar for Public Security, Emil Eichhorn, abolished the political police division of the Berlin police headquarters. Soon after, the political police sections of the Länder police forces were also abolished. These reforms were a direct result of the Social Democratic politicians' intense dislike for the snooping and provocation to which they had personally been subjected by the old imperial police services. The transformation of Germany into a semi-federal republic had the additional effect of lessening the normal collaboration between the police services, and, of course, had the important side effects of dispersing the police powers across the Länder, and within the Länder, among large numbers of local authorities.

Within a short space of time, however, operational realities led to the secret re-establishment in Prussia of a political police section, since it was clear that in the turbulent early days of the Weimar Republic a government deprived of political intelligence would be submerged in a wave of terror and counter-revolution. But since the re-establishment would offend the political principles of the Social Democrats, the re-emergence of the political police as a separate entity was disguised by nominally attaching them as a sub-section, known as Abteilung IA, of a general police department in Berlin. Other Länder secretly followed suit, often on the initiative of the administration and unknown to the local politicians. But the centralization of political police affairs remained very tenuous. The central state police desk in Abteilung IA was given primary responsibility for counter-espionage, by which was meant, at that stage, ensuring that the German armaments, forbidden by the Versailles Treaty, remained undiscovered. This special counter-espionage desk managed, because of its purpose, to obtain the co-operation and assistance of its opposite numbers in the political police sections in the Länder.

After the National Socialist regime's access to power in 1933 a new police system began to be organized. In Berlin, Diels, the head of the Prussian political police branch, was appointed director of Abteilung IA by Goering at the beginning of 1933. This section moved to new and separate headquarters in Prinz-Albrecht-strasse, and the law of April 26, 1933 formally established the secret state police, the Geheimestaatspolizei (Gestapo), 'to deal with political police tasks in parallel with or in place of the normal police authorities'. This law provided for subordinate field offices, and established the new Gestapo as a *Land* authority directly responsible to the Prussian minister of the interior. Its headquarters were the same as those of Abteilung IA. Formally, the field offices of the Gestapo were to be subordinate to the *Regierungspraesident* (the civil regional prefect), but in fact the law was so drafted that his instructions and tutelage could be overruled at will by the minister, or by the Gestapo officers themselves if they considered it operationally necessary.

In Bavaria, the other chief locus of police activities and the home of the National Socialist movement, Himmler was appointed acting *Polizeipraesident* in March 1933 by the Reich Commissar for Political Affairs, and his subordinate Reinhard Heydrich, until then head of the party's SD security service, became head of the Bavarian political police branch. Shortly afterwards Himmler, as Munich's Polizeipraesident, was nominated political adviser to the Bavarian Ministry of the Interior and all the political police sections throughout Bavaria were put under his control. This was followed by the creation of a special post, Political Police Commander of the State, for Himmler to fill. He was given formal authority over all the political police services in Bavaria, and these were detached from the Bavarian Ministry of the Interior to form a separate administration. Himmler was given his own logistic support, authority to requisition officers from other police formations for his own operational requirements, and control of 'existing and future concentration camps'.

One by one the other Länder followed suit, first formalizing the authority of the political police sections, which were now regarded as field offices of the Gestapo. Next they were detached from the normal state administration and given both administrative and political autonomy outside the control of the normal civil service, and then all the political police sections were amalgamated under the command of Himmler, as Political Police Commander. And throughout Germany Länder governments began to follow the example of Prussia where a ministerial ordinance permitted the police to operate without regard to the legal restrictions on their activities imposed by the Prussian administrative police law, one of the essential features of the Rechsstaat.

In Prussia the nominal attachment of the Gestapo to the Ministry of the Interior was ended in November 1933, and it was placed directly under the office of Minister-President Goering. In April 1934 Himmler was appointed deputy chief and inspector of the Prussian Secret State Police, and Heydrich in his turn chief of the Berlin Gestapo office. Their subordination to Goering was, in practice, very slight, and it is safe to say that by April 1934 in Prussia the Gestapo was an independent branch of the administration covering all police activities, standing apart from, but superior to, all other police authorities. And it had available to it all the criminal police files of the normal police services.

The tone began to alter. Goering could threaten (July 24, 1934) that 'should anyone in the future knowingly lift his hand against a member of the National Socialist party, or of the State, he should know, as of now, that he will promptly lose his life. It will be sufficient to show that he harboured the intention of committing the offence, or that, if he was acting under some compulsion, he had not been wholly effective, and had simply wounded when he had intended to kill.'[5] A certain constitutional rectitude was, however, preserved. A sympathetic jurist added the gloss that 'the term terror must once again have its proper place in the Penal Code'.[6] The laws relating to public order, economic offences and political subversion were strengthened, making the judiciary formal if reluctant aides of the new state. The definition of a political offence was broadened to include anti-governmental and anti-party activities as well as the traditional anti-constitutional offences.

These incursions into the judicial field continued into 1935. In Prussia it was held that the local administrative courts—one of the distinguishing features of the Rechtsstaat—'are not competent to examine the orders and affairs of the Secret Police'. Shortly afterwards another administrative court ruled that 'protective custody' was a form of arrest by the secret police made under emergency powers sufficient to exclude the courts from enquiring into the procedure. A Saxon administrative court accepted the argument of the police authorities that 'since businesses might be used as a cover for subversive activities, trade licenses should only be issued by local authorities after police approval'.[7] The effect of this was to put the livelihood of trades-men and professional people into the hands of the secret police, with all the consequent pressures that could be exerted upon them.

Himmler consolidated his various posts as political police commander of the various Länder by requiring the local police authorities to co-operate with the central political police bureau in Berlin, issuing for this purpose identical instructions to all the forces under his command. The law of February 10, 1936 further strengthened his hand. It laid down that the duty of the Gestapo was 'to investigate and suppress all anti-state tendencies through-out Prussia, to assemble and evaluate the results of any unrest, to keep the State informed, to keep other authorities abreast of any conclusions of importance to them, and to put forward sug-gestions. The Chief of the Gestapo in agreement with the Minister of the Interior will lay down in detail the duties to be transferred to the Gestapo.' The last sentence indicates that the civil service tried to keep some ministerial control over the activities of the Gestapo, and the law attempted to make it clear that the field offices of the Gestapo were not only responsible to the higher Gestapo offices but 'are at the same time subordinate to the Regierungspraesident concerned, will conform to his in-structions, and will keep him informed of all political police matters. The Head of the Stapostelle [the local office] is at the same time the Regierungspraesident's expert political adviser.'[8] But this attempt by the civil service to keep some control over the Gestapo's activities was entirely in vain, a mere exercise in theory. In practice the Regierungspraesident had a duty to obey the Gestapo in all matters that the Gestapo con-sidered of state importance, and Gestapo offices could give orders directly to all police services in the area, referring them directly to a superior Gestapo office rather than to the civil administration. The Gestapo drew this unwritten authority from the fact that it worked according to 'special principles and requirements' as opposed to the civil administration's 'general and regularly legalized rules', and the authority for it acting in this way stemmed from Hitler as Führer of the German people, and not from Hitler as chancellor.

The decree of June 17, 1936, signed by Hitler and Frick, the Reich minister of the interior, appointed Himmler chief of the German police and head of the SS (*Reichsführer-SS-und-Chef der Deutschen Polizei*). This decree unified control of police duties in the Reich and gave Himmler as police chief the direction and executive authority over all police matters within the competence of the Reich/Prussian Ministry of the Interior. In one move the entire German police apparat was not only centralized under Himmler's control as chief of the national police, but the police apparat as such was now yoked irrevocably to the SS, which had started out as the party's private security force, and to the Gestapo. Once again the attempts by the civil service to maintain some kind of constitutional authority over the police came to nothing, except for a compromise in the wording of the decree. Himmler was temporarily refused ministerial rank, but he was to be allowed to attend cabinet meetings when police affairs were under discussion. But since Heydrich (who conducted the preliminary discussions with the ministry) considered that 90 per cent of all administrative matters were the concern of the police, the price that was paid was very low.

Himmler promptly fashioned the police into his own instrument. Two decrees of June 26, 1936, fundamentally changed the nature of the police system and abolished the remnants of the federal structure. Essentially these decrees divided the police activities into two categories: the *Ordnungspolizei*, the regular uniformed police, the riot police, the Gendarmerie, the frontier police and the municipal police, responsible for public order in the conventional sense of the word; and the *Sicherheitspolizei*, the security police, which became responsible for the whole gamut of criminal, security, intelligence and secret police work. The Sicherheitspolizei was under Heydrich's authority, and thus became not only an independent power in its own right, but the political police had at their disposal all the resources, personnel, files and operational skills of the criminal police. Its all-embracing responsibility included passports, identity cards, surveillance of groups regarded as hostile or dangerous to the state, concentration camps, counter-espionage and the press, in addition to normal police investigation work.

The final stage in the centralization of the police services came with the absorption of the party's intelligence organizations with the police apparat. The most powerful of these, although in decline, was Heydrich's *Sicherheitsdienst*. This organization was joined with Sicherheitspolizei, under Heydrich, in September 1939 to form a combined security and political police organization for the whole of Germany and, later, of the occupied territories. The amalgamation was the last great institutional change designed to consolidate the police as one of the chief state authorities and leading apparat in internal affairs. The new body was styled the *Reichssicherheitshauptamt* (RSHA), Reich Security Headquarters. It obtained a huge store of police files and intelligence from the party apparat, and it took over the Sicherheitsdienst's foreign intelligence department, and its special concern for the investigation of opposition movements and internal German currents of opinion. The RSHA expanded considerably during the war, with specialist desks covering foreign countries, opposition groups and resistance movements, the employment of foreign workers, the extermination of Jewish populations and the dark empire of the concentration camps.

But this enormous power was still in the future. The creation of the Reich Security Headquarters in 1939 was the point at which Germany was transformed into a 'modern police state'. This transformation was accomplished despite the civil service, the judiciary, and the army, the three great established apparats of the German state. They regarded each other as pillars of society, supreme in their own fields, guardians of the best traditions of the country. They also traditionally regarded the police as a useful but essentially common subordinate body, loyal, unbending, obedient, and helpful as aides, informants and enforcement officers. Yet by 1939 the police apparat had emerged as the leading state authority in internal government, and by any standards had to be regarded as a powerful political force in its own right, independent in its own field, pursuing its own policies, possessing its own sources of power.

The growth of the police apparat to such a position transformed a country into a modern police state. We turn now, therefore, to analysing Himmler's administrative politics and his methods of institutional combat.

The German civil service, army and judiciary represented as formidable a combined administrative opposition as could be mustered at that time in any European country. The army and the civil service were noted for their high professional skills, and for their loyalty and obedience to their leaders. They had a high *esprit de corps*, although in some parts of the civil service this had been weakened by the politicking of the Weimar Republic. Both corps had a well-established professional ethic, and they were not easily intimidated.

Himmler managed from an early stage to achieve in his dealings with other groups a psychological dominance by his use of violence and his deliberate creation of an atmosphere of dread and foreboding, which his police came to epitomize. But although this must have touched individual civil servants, officers and judges in their secret hearts there is little evidence to suggest any wholesale collapse of morale within these groups. Until late in the war the activities of the police were seriously and formally questioned by other administrative authorities, both civil and military. It has been far too easy to assume that the German civil service and army succumbed to the terror of Himmler's police, or acted throughout the National Socialist regime as if they were frightened rabbits. They did not disarm easily.

The first to succumb was the judiciary. It was not the best in Europe, and many of its best members preferred the pleasures of academic jurisprudence to the responsibilities of the bench. The profession was perhaps better known in Europe for the subtlety and imagination of its theories than for the trenchancy and liberalism of its judges. None the less it was a strong, worthy organization and the National Socialist party, (in common with the opinions of the judiciary held by radical movements in other countries), regarded it with suspicion as too staid, conservative and lacking in revolutionary fervour.

We have already mentioned some of the devices which were used to neutralize the judiciary. As with all judges, the German bench accepted that the written law must be applied, provided that it is clearly stated and had passed through the correct and recognized procedure for reaching the statute book. Hitler was meticulous in providing legal grounds and support for everything he did. The new, stronger laws on public order, on political offences, on economic crimes, all had impeccable constitutional origins.

The judiciary was also the victim of the 'new philosophy'. It will be remembered that this doctrine, in so far as it could be understood, held that Hitler drew his formal authority over the state machinery of government from his position as Reich's chancellor, but that he also possessed extra-constitutional authority deriving from his role as Führer of the German people. He could at will assign state authority to the activities of other groups within the state, or cover their activities with an official seal. For the judiciary, the new philosophy meant, as Huber put it: 'legality is of significance as a formal bridge spanning the gulf which in fact exists between two systems basically different in nature [the authority of the state and the authority of the Führer] ... The legality method was adopted really with an eye to the technical functioning of the judicial and administrative systems.'[9]

The judiciary was therefore obliged to apply draconian laws, unexceptionable in their origins and clearly enforceable in constitutional terms. Combined with this was a parallel system of jurisprudence which, if it could be properly understood, justified recourse to a higher jurisprudence which recognized no formal procedures or legitimate boundaries. The traditional judiciary was consequently neutralized by the sophisticated use of verbalism, formalism and violence.

New institutional provisions ensured its complete subordination. Special 'People's Courts', under the control of the party and the police, were created to deal with a variety of new offences. The traditional powers of the police to inflict summary punishments were greatly strengthened and critical aspects of police administration, which had been put under the jurisdiction of administrative courts when the Rechtsstaat had come into being, were once again removed from judicial control, with reference back to the older practices of the traditional police state. In this way, not only was a parallel system of jurisprudence built up, but a parallel system for the administration of justice was created, in which whole areas of jurisdiction were removed from the control of the normal judiciary and put in the hands of the police apparat, or bodies dominated by its services. The final elimination of the judiciary as a serious check on the police can be precisely dated to January 25, 1938, when a directive was issued giving the Gestapo power of protective custody in the following terms: 'Protective custody can be decreed by the Secret State Police as a coercive method against those who endanger the safety of the people and the state by their attitude, in other words to break any chance of a revolt by the enemies of the people and the state.' There was no appeal against orders of protective custody.

The civil service had the longest unbroken tradition of administrative government in Europe, and it could trace its origins directly to the original Polizeistaat in Prussia. It was authoritative, paternalistic and conservative. The Weimar Republic's insistence that its members should break their personal oath of loyalty to the emperor, and its acceptance of political activity by civil servants in parliament, had to some extent damaged its ethos. But it still regarded order, predictability, welfare, deference and the higher national good as perfectly acceptable ideals. It was hardly likely, as an institution, to be greatly disturbed by the advent of strong central government, nor by inroads into the power of the legislatures, the trade unions and political parties, and it would very likely have preferred a consciously cultured but not politically inspired press.

The civil service would probably have been prepared actively to co-operate with a new paternalist government. The National Socialist theory of the state, however, saw the civil service as an instrument subordinate to the will of the Führer and the control of the party. For the civil service it was one thing to obey orders and work for the national good—it was another to condone the excesses of wild and irresponsible men, using the state apparatus for the most questionable and violent ends. Civil servants were no doubt subjected to the same pressures of personal intimidation as other German citizens, and, within the service, the traditional right of the government to appoint freely to the highest administrative posts allowed the National Socialist party to put trusted men in strategic posts. The dichotomy between party and state introduced by the new philosophy did, however, have one positive result: the state authorities, by implication, would normally operate within the known rules of administrative law.

These rules were founded in a long tradition of orderly, comprehensive and structured government, and they did not lend themselves to the permanently arbitrary form of administration which the new philosophy required. In individual cases the machinery could be used to pervert the natural course of administration and administrative justice, but within the bureaucratic structure, taken as a whole, impulsive and *ad hoc* solutions remained exceptional, and were regarded as such. The effect of the party on the civil service remained restricted.

Nevertheless the civil service's political power which it had guarded and husbanded for so long was captured by the rising police apparat. There was no head-on conflict between them, but there was always in the background the constant efforts of individual leaders of the state to gain positions of power. Himmler's greatest asset was his professed loyalty and unconditional support for Hitler and he and his police owed no loyalty to the state or to its institutions. Himmler made the police into the executive power for the Führer's personal authority. They therefore did not accept the state's laws, administrative procedures or constitutional limitations. Their one unalterable duty was to make effective the Führer's will. The German police apparat, dominated by the political police, was led outside the normal functioning of the state. It was diverted from its normal defensive duties to society of protecting the state, property and individuals, to an offensive role devoted to satisfying political needs. It became a para-state organization with its own mission and its own loyalties. It was concerned with the formal police powers of the state in so far as they were necessary for the fulfilment of its primary political purpose.

Himmler's great weapon was the claim of administrative necessity, which all bureaucrats can understand. He could accept the formal subordination of parts of his police service to the civil administration, while at the same time being in a position to evade control when he considered it necessary. He always provided himself with an escape route which allowed the police to refer directly to their superior in the police hierarchy whenever 'operational requirements' made this necessary. Thus, during the evolution of the regime into a modern police state, Himmler was prepared to accept reality and let the civil service have the form. By elevating the political police to a position of supremacy within the police apparat itself, he covered the operations of the entire police service with the special requirements of operational security and administrative secrecy which could reasonably be required for the political police. The political police offered 'the greatest scope, or at least the most convenient justification, for secret processes, unauthorized executive measures, and deviation from normal rules'.[10] In practice, then, the police apparat defeated the civil service by circumventing the normal state apparatus rather than by conquering it. Himmler used the army's favourite field exercise of encirclement to win this victory.

The army was, in a sense, Himmler's greatest problem. He had not only to re-establish the state's monopoly of physical coercion, which the National Socialist cohorts and their enemies had destroyed under the Weimar Republic, but he had to ensure that, when re-established, the police rather than the army would emerge as the regime's Praetorian Guard.

After 1918 there were two sources of *esprit de corps* within the German military and para-military forces. There remained the traditional discipline of the professional military with its *hauteurs*, its *grandeurs* and its *misères*. But a new ideology of arms had arisen, that of the *Freikorps*, the freebooters, the ideological warriors, whose life and ethos were reminiscent of the Renaissance gangs in Italy. The National Socialist movement early acquired its own private army, the *Sturmabteilung*, built on local units, responsible for protecting the party's own meetings and personalities and for wrecking those of other groups. In 1925 there was a disagreement between Hitler and Röhm, its leader, about the proper function of this force. Hitler wished it to be completely subordinate to the part leadership and used for political indoctrination and civil disturbance; Röhm wished to maintain its (his) independence as a support force able to intervene violently whenever necessary. Röhm wished in fact to be able to continue his sometimes equivocal understandings with other Freikorps units and with the army.

In reply Hitler organized a para-military force tightly bound by personal loyalty to himself as the Führer, and entirely dependent upon him as party leader. He used his embryonic personal guard, the *Stabswach*. Further units of the same kind were recruited from the party's most active and loyal supporters and formed into protection squads, the *Schutzstaffeln* (SS). It was not intended to rival the Sturmabteilungen (SA) as a mass organization, but to provide protection for Hitler and other party dignitaries, and to defend the party and its organization against attack. Soon after, with the SA reorganized under central direction, the new SS lost some of its importance, until Himmler took it over in 1939, expanded it, and reformed its cadres. The SS then assumed duties of a police nature within the party, and not only provided bodyguards but also built up a counter-espionage service to keep a watching brief on other parties.

In 1932 both the SA and the SS were briefly banned, but by 1933 the SS had grown to number about 50,000 men. Its counter-intelligence and intelligence duties were placed under the command of a special section within the SS, the Sicherheitsdienst, commanded by Heydrich and at first known as the 'I.c Service', which, as we have seen, was finally amalgamated with the other police services in 1939.

Just before coming to power Hitler again reorganized the SS, creating small commando units for special duties, including a personal bodyguard for himself. These sections formed the cadres of general service troops, which developed into the Waffen-SS divisions, which were entirely military in character. They were militarized combat units which, during the war were widely used as crack frontline troops. But they were also, as Himmler intended them to be, the shock troops of the regime, owing their loyalty to himself and to the regime, rather than normal army divisions owing their loyalty to the general staff and the army commanders.

Thus, from the beginning the National Socialist government possessed its own armed forces, parallel to, and independent of, the army. Himmler regarded his SS troops as the élite corps of the regime, and it always provided him with a counterforce of entirely loyal troops on whom he could rely should the military leaders attempt to use the forces under their command against the Führer or the regime.

Until very late in the day this was unnecessary, as Hitler

played most skilfully on the army's traditions, guarded its pre-rogatives and privileges, and separated it from the normal functioning of the political system. He extracted from soldiers a personal oath of loyalty, which meant a good deal in the traditions of the German army; but, basically, Hitler's skill was of a simpler kind: he provided the army with a purpose, and kept it occupied, as a child can be distracted by something which pops away from something which burns.

Himmler's police apparat was tacitly accepted by the army as one of the leading state apparats in 1938 when, contrary to normal custom and the understanding of The Hague conventions, the police were formally empowered to move in with the army into Austria and Czechoslovakia to assume responsibility for the internal order of those countries. This could just be explained away in these cases with the argument that these territories were an integral part of the Greater Reich, but in 1939 the police were given all responsibility in Poland for security behind the lines, and assumed direct executive command as soon as fighting ceased. Himmler's agents infiltrated the army's Field Police (responsible for provost duties and special investigations in the command area), and although this force remained technically under the high command, its operations in occupied territories were officially conducted under the authority of the head of the Gestapo. It is clear that the police operated in many cases without the knowledge of the army. Himmler simply used his proven device of running an administration parallel to the normal state administration to protect his officers from outside control and investigation.

We have now reached the point where we can briefly summarize in analytical terms what happened within the German state between 1933 and 1939 to transform it into a modern police state. It had two of the characteristic bases of the traditional police state. First, it professed a positive, interventionist philosophy, which had as its ultimate purpose the mobilization, modernization and welfare of society. (These terms were defined by National Socialists in a highly idiosyncratic way, but for our analysis we can afford, at this stage, to ignore that.) Second, it was an authoritarian regime, by which we simply mean that the landmarks of liberal democratic regimes had been abolished. That is, parliament, press, trade unions, education, the electorate, and, up to a point, personal liberty were subject to the control of central authorities.

It has been cogently argued, however, that the elimination of political dissent in an authoritarian regime does not abolish internal opposition as such. Dissent is replaced by factional and institutional rivalries between competing state apparats. Administrative politics becomes a substitute for 'political' politics. It was this new feature in state organization which led to the modern police state diverging from the classic pattern of the traditional police state. Whereas the older version was based upon a simple triad of power—the single directing political will, the civil service and the army—a century's development had introduced new power centres, and a dissemination of political authority. What happens in a modern police state is that these dispersed sources of power are once again knitted together, captured by a new state institution—the police apparat—and used to establish a dominant position in determining the internal policy of a country.

There are two main arenas in which this struggle for dominance is conducted. One area of conflict is within the police apparat itself. The stages are clearly marked. First, the police services are centralized under effective national command; second, the political police service is built up into a national service with its own powers and chain of command, parallel to the normal criminal and uniformed police services; next, the political police service is amalgamated with the criminal police service, with the political police in command; the uniformed police services are then subordinated to the needs and special operational requirements of the unified political/criminal police service; and, finally, the uniformed police service is strengthened as an armed reserve force by the creation of a para-military force with its own weapons, intelligence and logistic support, under the command of, and loyal to, the central police command. The policies laid down by the central police command are now dictated by political requirements and are designed to make the police apparat as a whole into an offensive weapon of the state rather than a protective force for society. Its main concern is now the control and formulation of state policy in internal affairs rather than the implementation of objective law and the protection of private and collective rights.

The second arena in which this contest takes place is that of the central government. Here the police apparat as a whole challenges the other state institutions which limit its freedom of action in internal affairs. The judiciary is neutralized to prevent police policies being hampered by the formalism of the law, or by the intrusion of other standards and criteria of judgement. The police apparat obtains sufficient judicial powers in its own right to operate independently in fields which it comes unilaterally to define as matters of criminal procedure, and establishes its own parallel jurisdiction.

The police apparat encroaches upon the police powers of the civil service in order to obtain administrative leverage in areas critical to its interests, or which are useful in enabling it to penetrate into society at large. It creates a parallel system of administration exempt from normal bureaucratic rules, and covers its activities with appeals to administrative necessity to justify wholly discretionary procedures.

The army's fundamental power of monopolizing the physical means of coercion is then broken by the creation of a para-military police service, independent of the army's chain of command, and owing its loyalty to leaders in the police apparat, outside the control of the military hierarchy.

When the contest in these two arenas has reached a conclusion favourable to the police apparat a modern police state has been created. It differs in important respects from its predecessor, the traditional police state, and it falls short of what it may become, the totalitarian police state. But before we turn to this later development we should deal with two subsidiary matters.

6 / Police Methods

It is unrealistic to ignore the special feeling of dread that the modern term 'police state' now evokes. This dread seems to arise from unanalysed fears that police powers will be systematically abused, and police services and their agents will behave in an especially intimidating manner. These preoccupations were seldom noticed in the traditional police state where the principal fears expressed were of clandestine and persistent spying, which was much resented, and where there was a belief that the police used their offices for interfering in politics. The police were regarded as being the willing tools of the executive, but it was against the executives and the authoritarian systems of government rather than against the police themselves that the hostility was chiefly aimed.

What seems to have been the principal change in the modern police state is the emergence of the police service as an offensive force, reversing its traditional role as defender of the existing order and protector of the state. This change involves the systematic and deliberate use of police powers to alter the nature of the state, and to convert people to views different from those they previously held—or, at the very least, to ensure that in their public behaviour and private conversations they act as if they do hold these new views. In the modern police state the police come to regard political re-education as an important part of their functions.

Now, the trouble is that spying, brutality, arbitrary use of power and preparedness to take the law into their own hands is an integral part of the nature of any police system and their incidence cannot be taken as a simple definition of a 'police state'. It might, perhaps, be helpful to make this point in a detailed and documented way.

First, there is the arbitrary nature of police powers. No matter how much police powers are formally controlled by an insistence on due process, objective expert evidence or independent arbitration, their application, which is the work of the police services, is essentially arbitrary. Most states today find themselves with a battery of laws of exception passed in the sometimes distant past to deal with particular crises. As the crises passed, the laws have fallen into desuetude, but they have rarely been removed from the statute books. Such laws of exception provide a potential armoury for police authorities to use if they need them, or think they need them.

Furthermore, it is clear that no matter how tightly drawn laws may be in theory, in practice their operation is haphazard and uncertain. It is part of the nature of contemporary police powers to be selective, and this, by definition, involves choice. The complexity of administration in modern societies is such that if all laws and police ordinances were to be universally enforced, all citizens would be criminals. The modern tendency of legislators, as well as administrators, to attempt to improve society by penal sanctions has led to a situation in which anti-social behaviour is combated by rules to make such activity technically illegal as well as socially repugnant. One result of this has been that the law designed to protect society against the rich man in his mansion can can also be used to persecute the poor man in his cottage.

Police power in a contemporary setting has largely become the institutionalized use of society's discretionary powers, and the application of the law, although not the law itself, becomes relativistic. The foundations for a modern police state are often if inadvertently laid by social reformers.

We can summarize this argument by referring to counsel's speech in the case of Regina *v.* Commissioner of Metropolitan Police *ex parte* Blackburn. Mr. Blackburn, a former member of Parliament had been attempting for some time to force the Metropolitan Police to 'prosecute known and repeated breaches of the Gaming Acts in London extending over a lengthy period'. There was adequate evidence to show that such breaches had occurred. Before the Court of Appeal counsel for the police argued that

> ... as a matter of law, mandamus would not issue against a chief officer of police in respect of any matter in the appeal because the Commissioner had no legal duty to Mr. Blackburn: he had a discretion in regard to them. The Commissioner could not be forced to prosecute because he had no duty to do so. The fact that no duty existed to prosecute was correlative in English law and practice with the right of all citizens to prosecute. Counsel said that he had been unable to find a decision which imposed a duty on a chief officer of police to prosecute. If there was any duty, it was owed to the Crown and not to any member of the public.[1]

What appears to happen in normal societies is that the exercise of police powers tends to be determined according to an intuitive sense of values, the police normally reflecting the values of society. Certain offences are deemed by the police to be so intrinsically harmful or hateful to society that they are automatically pursued with the greatest possible vigour. At the other end of the scale there are a host of trivial offences whose prosecution is purely random. They will be prosecuted if detected, if their authors are known, or, in some cases, if the police authorities wish to make an example. The police put their own gloss on the religious notion of mortal and venial sin. Mortal sin must not go undetected and unpunished; venial sin needs repentance but does not imperil the soul. Venial offences will be punished spasmodically in order to encourage people to obey the law in case they are caught. Few people, apart from professional criminals, understand theories of risk and probability in this context, and much of the effectiveness of police power lies in maintaining order and stability by unpredictability and uncertainty. By their action or inaction police authorities are permanently in a position to modify the real effects of the law by administrative action. They can quietly bury the 30 mph speed limit, but they can equally resurrect the medieval charge of 'making an affray'. A good deal of social jurisprudence is created by these means.

Second, we can look at the vexed question of police brutality. There is no doubt that the police power ultimately rests on the legitimate use of force. Physical coercion is one of the special attributes of the state, and police forces (and soldiers) are its agents in this respect. Charges of police brutality are of two kinds: private violence and public force, in both cases the charge being that the use of force exceeds that which is necessary to achieve the police purpose, or is exercised in illegitimate ways.

The illegitimate use of private violence is so widely documented that there is little point in discussing whether or not it occurs. It is normally associated with the interrogation of suspects on police premises, and it is not always clear at what stage the application of psychological pressure can be regarded as becoming an illegitimate use of force. Over the years, in civilized societies, the powers of interrogation have been restricted by legal guarantees to prevent extortion of confessions by violence, threats or inducements. The right to legal representation, to medical examination, to prompt and explicit charges, to a speedy appearance before a magistrate, to freedom from self-incrimination, have all found their place in codes of criminal procedure. The temptation for policemen to extort confessions can normally only be thwarted by these elaborate rules of conduct instilled into a force by good training, and enforced by the example of senior officers. The temptation to cut corners and obtain evidence by unorthodox or illegal means will always be strong, particularly when the police are dealing with known criminals. In the last resort, society often depends upon the common sense and scepticism of its judges, and on the entirely healthy tension which exists between the judiciary and the police services.

The use of public force by the police is apparently on the increase but this may very well be due to the widespread nature of the mass media, and the development of radical theories of confrontation with authorities. There are undoubtedly countries where policemen are for the most part of a rude, bullying and choleric disposition, but in societies where the police seek voluntary co-operation from the public, little benefit is to be gained by public hooliganism.

The spectacle of public brutality is never edifying, and is nearly always interpreted in conflicting ways according to the political sentiments of the observers. The use of force against students in Chicago is a wicked Fascist exercise: the use of force against students in Prague is a wicked Communist act. The facile nature of these judgements is not infrequently due to the unconscious lack of perspective obtained from viewing highlights of a few local scuffles, without being aware of the mounting tensions and provocations which precede the incidents. The intentions of the leaders of demonstrations and riots are frequently as important as the orders of police officers or methods of police deployment. A crowd in a mood is always dangerous, and always unpredictable. A peaceful demonstration can become a riot through the activities of a dozen persons carrying darts, marbles or stones. Police forces are always conscious of being in a minority, and aware that their personal safety depends upon their cohesion. It takes considerable experience to judge when the mood of a crowd has subtly shifted from good-natured turbulence to unified hostility, and to know the moment when the mass has reached its critical point and menace becomes attack.

Police tactics recommend that a smaller, disciplined force should always try to keep the initiative in difficult situations, and if necessary to strike before a crowd becomes a mob with a single motive. This judgement has to be made under conditions of growing tension, overt acts of violence, and the awareness that the police cannot run away although their opponents can. If they break they remain marked men because of their uniform, and policemen in violent countries remember the fate of the AVRO men in Budapest in 1956.

This atmosphere, as well as the political mistakes always liable in decisions concerning the use of force, is well conveyed in a report of events in Battapaglia in southern Italy, in March 1969. The city's principal economic activity, a state tobacco factory, was threatened with closure and the workers decided on a peaceful protest demonstration. It remained peaceful until a young police official ordered a police squad to charge to clear a railway crossing, and the Ministry of the Interior, far away in Rome, sent orders for the police to clear the streets. A police riot squad of 180 men which attempted to do so was driven out of the city by the crowd, leaving about 100 police besieged in the central police commissariat. The Ministry of the Interior promised reinforcements, and recommended that in the meantime the police should make periodic sorties to relieve the pressure upon them. The crowd began to increase until some observers estimated it at 3,000 people. During one of the sorties policemen became separated from their companions, and were set upon by the crowd. One or two began to fire wildly in a panic, and a school-teacher and a boy were killed.

The crowd now began to storm the commissariat in earnest, setting fire to the adjacent town hall, destroying police vehicles and throwing Molotov cocktails through the windows of the commissariat. An observer reported that 'the crowd cried furiously to the besieged police "Surrender, come out with your hands up, or we will burn you alive". What is not so well known is that during each of the sorties made by the police only two or three returned to the commissariat out of the ten or fifteen who had left. The others took to the fields, hid in shops, in the cemetery, in friendly houses . . .' The same observer was told by one of the policemen who remained in the commissariat that they were convinced they would be killed like rats. 'There were about forty of us, perhaps fewer. Some were weeping, some were swearing, others were preparing to throw away their uniforms. One of us, despite the dark, wrote a will for his wife. Towards the end, when the reinforcements had still not arrived, the police commissioner gave orders to distribute sub-machine guns and rifles, with three magazines apiece, to each man, and, on command, to fire at sight at the first people who might get in.'[2]

This atmosphere of tension and near hysteria has been repeated in a dozen countries in the past year and, indeed, the evidence of a police sergeant in Ulster would be not dissimilar to this account. When a police force moves to break up a riot unpredictable forces are released. In conditions of mob violence exceptional reserves of discipline, training and obedience are required; without them lives are lost and heads broken. The more the demonstration has armed itself for trouble, or itself resorts to unconventional tactics, the more police forces, if they are competent, will attempt to keep their advantage by resorting to specialized armaments, and, in the last resort, lethal weapons.

Third in our analysis of police methods we have the case of a normally disciplined force which, for higher motives, as it sees it, resorts to patently illegal activities. The police force becomes a law unto itself. There are, in the nature of things, few documented examples of this, although the actions of the police 'Death Squad' in Brazil in eliminating criminals who have been left free as a result of political or judicial corruption, are beginning to enter this category. But the following is one account which is historically illustrative.

At the time of the first anarchist outrages in Paris in 1893 the police authorities were concerned by the legislature's apparent lack of resolve in providing adequate laws to quell the increasing tendency of public opinion to endow the anarchist movement with a certain romanticism rather than to see its activities as unbridled violence. On November 9, 1893, an anarchist, Vaillant, entered the Chamber of Deputies and threw an infernal machine into the assembly. It caused little damage, and people remarked at the coolness of the president who ruled that the debates should continue. The following day the Chamber passed an act limiting freedom of expression. The biography of a senior policeman at that time clearly suggests that the bomb was made in the laboratories of the Paris police, and that Vaillant was given benevolent assistance in his attempt.[3]

The following year President Carnot was assassinated, and further restrictive measures were passed by the Chamber. A sentimental fringe of liberal society still saw in the anarchist movement a certain lyricism and an idealistic demand for freedom from outworn customs and habits. A M. Puibaraud was appointed director of research on special service in the prefecture of police and within a few weeks

> ... one could no longer take a step in Paris without finding sardine tins filled with green powder in the way. The concierges found them in the morning in front of their lodgings, on the staircases in the apartment houses, and in dustbins. It is unlikely they could have exploded, but they put the fear of God into the inhabitants.
>
> These tins were taken with infinite precaution to the municipal police laboratory, and the following day the newspapers reported that they had been extremely dangerous. Some did blow up, but in places where they never seemed to harm anyone, for instance, in an out of the way urinal, or a deserted cul-de-sac. And, as if to punish him, a bomb blew up in the face of the poet Tailhade, who had written a poem on the beauty of *la Geste*, one evening while he was dining Chez Fayot. The public which had been willing to applaud the exploits of the Anarchists as spectators, were the first to demand that the game should be stopped as soon as they felt their own skins to be in danger.[4]

Next we must consider the question of police spying. Again, in the nature of things, there is very little contemporary documentation for this. It is frequently associated in the public mind with a 'secret' or a 'political' police service, as if forces of this kind are in themselves an affront to liberal dignity. In the natural course of events much police work has to be kept secret. Even the most liberal chief constable in Britain would refuse to discuss with his watch committee all his operational plans and contingency arrangements.

A distinction is sometimes drawn between the laudable activity of protecting society, and the obnoxious activity of collecting political secrets, but this is largely to ignore the realities of state interests. Police obtain information about plots, conspiracies, subversion and espionage because they have a duty to protect the state as it exists. To do this they are inevitably concerned with any activity, overt or secret, which might undermine the fabric of the state. (The irony of the abolition of the political police in the Weimar Republic was that as a direct consequence the reforming Social Democrats put the state more firmly into the hands of the army and the Freikorps, and left the field clear for all the clandestine and anti-republican activities which greatly benefited the National Socialists.) The work is essentially informative in character; it is the acquisition of information rather than the detection of crime. The information is to allow the police to ring the alarm bell rather than to put out the fire. Inevitably much of this work touches people who have little intention of engaging in illegal activities and have no clearly stated subversive ends. The police simply argue that it takes time to know, and that the price of security is eternal vigilance.

The crux of the matter is that certain police intelligence work is justified, and some is not. Only rarely can operations of this kind be analysed by the outsider, but one historical example, and one more recent occurrence, can point the contrast.

In the records of the Archives Nationales[5] in Paris it is possible to piece together some idea of the unceasing watch the police maintained on that extraordinary variety of enemies of the state under the Third Republic: anarchists, royalists, syndicalists, priests, soldiers and politicians. The police records show how the police systematically infiltrated their own agents into these circles, or, more frequently, hired informants. These *correspondants* had only one master, an inspector of police, and they remain disguised under their code names. They parade before history as 'Londres', 'Metz', 'Victor', 'Lutetia', 'Nazareth', 'Arnaud', 'Louis', 'Lazare' and so on.

The morning after a secret meeting of the *Conseil Ouvrier* a report from a participant was in police headquarters. A document concerning the *Union des Syndicats* was sequestrated 'since it might appear interesting, for under the heading of expenditure in the accounts there is a sum of 77 francs 20 for the purchase of revolvers and cartridges'. The leader (as it turned out, a double-crossing rogue) of a royalist plot to kidnap the president of the republic disappeared with the money he had raised from royalist sympathizers for arms, and reappeared in Brussels, having a private lunch, fully reported, with one of his trusties, himself a correspondant.

'Victor' reported on a conversation with a grand lady who expressed fears of socialism, and adds, 'I was present at several conversations between foreign diplomats, and this was also their expressed opinion.' When the Duc d'Orléans was sounded out by the political bureau of the Royalist Party as to whether he had been approached recently about a new conspiracy against the republic, a correspondant was at his elbow to report to the prefecture that 'he replied, Certainly not, and that if any royalists, whether they are members of the Action Française or of other independent groups, were to come with propositions of this kind, he would order them to leave, and immediately call for his chauffeur, and the very same day put 300 to 400 kilometres distance between himself and these conspirators in whom he had no confidence.'

This is the stuff of good police intelligence. From one source there is advance notice of the possibility of clandestine armament; from another the proof that an apparent kidnapping plot of a serious political nature is in reality an elaborate confidence trick. It is always helpful to know the ebb and tide of public opinion, and it is of the highest importance to know the likely reactions of a key political figure in a delicate political situation. But it depends on the reliability of the 'correspondants', who can only be cross-checked up to a point, and on the discriminating use of few but reliable sources with a specific task to attend to.

This contrasts markedly with a modern example. In September 1966, the newly appointed head of the Italian counterespionage service discovered that a certain number of files could not be accounted for. These files were from the profile section, and they seemed to include the dossiers of several prominent politicians. Enquiries within the office suggested that they had been borrowed by the previous head of the service who had apparently taken them into his own possession. An internal commission of enquiry was set up, and in its report it disclosed that for the previous ten years the service had systematically built up a compendium of intelligence on politicians, scientists, state officials, serving officers, journalists, priests and bishops. This work had been done by means of 'tailing, the interception of letters and telephone communications, and the use of informers, at the cost of milliards of lire paid out of the secret funds of the counter-intelligence service. The organization had used an extremely large number of collaborators to be found in the most diverse and unexpected quarters. If the names of these informers were to be disclosed, public opinion would be disconcerted and shocked.'[6]

The systematic collection of material had increased enormously since this surveillance was begun, and the form in which it was handled had also changed. The information collected had altered in its nature as time went on, and, far from being concerned with matters of direct interest to the security police, it had come to be designed to provide particulars of peoples' lives which might make them vulnerable to pressure. It concentrated on business dealings, extra-marital relations, the birth of illegitimate children, sexual habits and appetites, and political connections. On several occasions the enquiries had extended to cover the family, servants and friends of the people concerned.

The commission of enquiry also found that the requests for this information had come directly from the central headquarters, and that the defence that local security sections had acted with an excess of zeal because of local political pressures was false. No political pressure to obtain this information had been proved. The commission found that the service 'had always operated free of all control, and it has therefore been able to develop in an improper manner its own activities beyond the limits of propriety and legality, without any responsible directive'.[7] The commission concluded that some surveillance would always be necessary over people or bodies whose activities could reasonably cause concern as a possible threat to the state, and it also accepted that this surveillance might sometimes have to be extended to innocent persons who frequented circles which were themselves under suspicion. But it held that intelligence coverage of this kind became clearly illegitimate when it was systematically extended to cover everyone who had achieved some prominence in public life, and when information which had no conceivable relations to security matters was systematically collected and catalogued.

The way in which this counter-intelligence service operated shows two very clear dangers inherent in all political police work. First, a police system, like any other form of organization, tries to work towards self-government, setting its own norms, and controlling its own operations. The commission of enquiry specifically commented upon the resistance and reluctance of officials within the service to give evidence. One of the previous heads of the service, indeed, had formally to be recalled from the reserve so that he could be officially ordered to give evidence. Second, the acquisition and utilization of confidential information for purposes extraneous to its proper police purpose is always a standing temptation to politicians, and to a certain kind of official. This danger increases the more a political system is unstable.

Now it can be seen that those elements which we most closely identify as being properties of a modern police state are, in fact, potentialities of any police system. The arbitrary use of police powers, brutality, spying, secrecy, the temptation to act as a law unto itself are characteristics inherent in every police system. They stem from the very nature of police work. It is also clear that modern technological changes have increased the possibility of abuse. Charging with batons is very old fashioned as compared to the use of tear gas, and far more dangerous to the police; the punch-up in the cells is far less effective than the use of electricity; the interception of communications has altered its nature since the days when it was necessary to open letters, (an art, incidentally, so refined in Britain in the nineteenth century that Napoleon III sent his police officers to study the methods used). And, as we said at the beginning of this chapter, the more societies make anti-social behaviour technically illegal, the greater the discretionary powers vested in the police authorities.

It can well be remarked that although the potential for police abuses exists in all states, it is a characteristic of civilized liberal democratic regimes that this potential, and the abuses, are kept under control. The knowledge of the potential is the key factor in causing common law countries to act with such circumspection whenever police powers are involved. It can then be remarked that the full blossoming of police powers and abuses can only occur in authoritarian regimes, and it is clear that authoritarian regimes run much greater dangers in this direction than liberal democratic regimes. But the curious fact is that several types of authoritarian regimes also manage to keep them under control. Many observers who express horror at the notion of a police state, justify the replacement of a corrupt democracy by a military regime. The regard in which Pakistan under Ayub

Khan was held by some western liberal observers was quite different from the bitter dislike they expressed for Nkrumah's police state in Ghana. In many cases, of course, what these observers accept as being a necessary process of discipline and mobilization is, if they knew it, acceptance of the virtues and benefits of the traditional police state as it was developed by the Cameralists in the old Polizeistaat. We have made the point, however, that it is unrealistic not to take into account the special pejorative sense in which the term police state is used nowadays. Why is it that the idea of police rule is so much more offensive than the idea of, say, military government?

7/Police Psychology

There seem to be two answers to the question asked at the end of the last chapter. First, there is a natural and instinctive reaction against what police power stands for. This is a fairly common human response and one which may be readily observed. Second, however, there is also the historical evidence of what happens to the police themselves if they acquire unbridled authority within a state, and it is as much this objective evidence as the instinctive reaction which creates public attitudes.

We need, indeed, spend little time on the question of instinctive reactions. Few people like authority unless they exercise it themselves. Objective authority is always a diminution of personality, a restriction on freedom of expression and a continual and implicit threat to personal dignity. The policeman is the personal embodiment of this authority. He is in the tradition of the parent, the schoolmaster and the sergeant-major, but he does not have the affection of the first, the improving quality of the second, or the glamour of the third. The policeman is the permanent censor of public behaviour in society, and as such can hardly be expected to be loved. Nor can he expect to be admired as the soldier is. The soldier appears to be concerned with the greatest end of all societies—its preservation. He has an implicit contract with society that he will put his life at stake to maintain the lives and security of others. The contract is immense, the man admirable, the life adventurous. The cult of the hero is deeply embedded, rightly or wrongly, in most human beings, and a little of the Victoria Cross rubs off on to every soldier. Furthermore, the great hours of most societies have been associated with military exploits: its achievements of independence from foreign rule or its defeat of a wicked enemy. The military in undeveloped countries has so frequently stepped in to prevent the internal collapse of society, or to rid the country of tyrants or demagogues, that it has sometimes seemed almost idealized as the bastion of the state, the only thoroughly responsible organization, or the only disciplined model for mobilizing for development.

The literature shows two different attitudes to the police which seem accurately to reflect public reactions to police work. The first is what might be termed the 'artisanal': the view that the police function is essentially workmanlike, pragmatic and plodding. Seen this way policemen are essentially working-class professionals, with authoritarian personalities, engaged in hard and uninspired labour keeping their equals in order. They are regarded in the same light as charge hands or leading seamen, directly descended from the old nightwatchman. Their experience reinforces their authoritarian personalities, and they can become disgruntled and conscious of 'status discrepancies', the feeling that no segment of society really appreciates their contribution to society or the risks they run. They are fundamentally amoral, as proved by the constantly observed phenomenon that professional policemen make the transition from one regime to another without difficulty. Their professional ethic discounts the ideological nature of the regime they are serving.[1] They are the descendants of the squirearchies' parish constables.

This view is supported by an account of police activities in the sociological classic, William Foot Whyte's *Street Corner Society*. Observation in his anonymous city indicated to him that the primary function of the police department was not the enforcement of law but the regulation of illegal activities. The 'good people' of Eastern City, who had written their moral judgements into law, demanded through their newspapers that the law be enforced. The people of Cornerville, at the other end of town, had different standards and had built up a social organization which depended upon freedom to violate the law. The local policeman had more in common with Cornerville people than with those who demanded law enforcement. Law enforcement had a direct effect upon Cornerville people whereas it only indirectly affected the 'good people' of the city.

> Under these circumstances the smoothest course for the officer is to conform to the social organisation with which he is in direct contact and at the same time to try to give the impression to the outside world that he is enforcing the law. He must play an elaborate role of make-believe, and, in so doing, he serves as a buffer between divergent social organisations with their conflicting standards of conduct. . . . By regulating [rackets] the officer can satisfy the demands for law enforcement with a number of token arrests and be free to make his adjustments to the local situation.[2]

The role of the untouchable policeman is important in this respect not because he represents virtue by being incorruptible but because he helps to keep the police organization in a state of equilibrium between the pressures which are exerted upon it from both sides. The untouchable policeman has to exist in order to protect the police organization from threats of outside intervention.

This account is convincing in its brisk reality. Whyte remarks, 'in dealing effectively with the police, money is important, but so are position and personal relations. Neither is effective without the other.'[3] He noted that middle-class people expected the law to be enforced without fear or favour, but that Cornerville people and many policemen themselves held the much more sophisticated view that the policeman should have the confidence of the people in his area so that many local difficulties might be settled by him in a personal way without making arrests. The highly legalistic view of the police function cuts the policeman off from personal relations, and prevents him from being a mediator in his area; but at the same time too much involvement prevents him from acting with the vigour prescribed by the law.

This is the 'artisanal' view of the police function. It is amoral, sceptical and down to earth. General observation suggests that many people accept these terms of reference when discussing police affairs, and that many policemen would accept this view as an unflattering but perceptive appreciation of one aspect of police work, the aspect with which the normal public habitually has contact.

But there is another attitude, and this is reflected in the same public's fascination with police stories of crime, detection and intrigue. This is the romantic view of the police function, and it goes directly back to the discovery by French novelists that the quirks and curiosities and mysteries of society can best be viewed through the eyes of policemen, the eternal observers of the human condition.

Throughout the nineteenth century the French, who had been deeply affected by the mysteries and plots associated with Fouché's police system, and its aftermath, used the police to elucidate their own society. Several editions of Vidocq's *Mémoires* regaled the public with the biography of an ex-convict who became director of the Sûreté, and who moved with equal ease in the low world and in high politics. His audience was told of the conspiracies of the secret police, of 'l'Épingle noire' of the plots of La Rochelle. The mysteries of the secret police became part of the French literary tradition. The power of the secret police was deliberately exaggerated in such books as *Le livre noir de Mm. Franchet et Delavau* in order to attack the Ultras and *le parti prêtre*. Eugène Sue described *Les mystères de Paris*, and Victor Hugo added his mysterious policeman, Javert.

The writers' preoccupation with the Paris underworld of revolutionary plots reflected the politicians' continual concern with the apparently unending intrigues by the opposition against the state. This atmosphere encouraged the continuance of Fouché's conception of police work, since the perpetual threat to the state suggested that the police were the last defence of society. Gisquet, a former prefect of police in Paris, undoubtedly reflected bourgeois public opinion when he said bluntly that the police mission was essentially political 'because all parties in turn could seize the supreme power, or at least attempt to do so, by violence. The government is like a fortress daily besieged and threatened by assault; one must always therefore be on the alert, always have one's eyes fixed on the enemy's movements. In such a situation the police is indispensable; it is the sentinel who watches over the common welfare.' He went on to say that the first duty of a prefect of police was to study society 'to find out where lies the danger and in what class are to be found the enemies whose manoeuvres must be watched and whose assaults must be forestalled or suppressed'.[4]

This mixture of romanticism, intrigue, mystery and danger led Balzac to ask his complex question with its surprising answer: What is the noblest profession? The answer, he said, was that of the policeman. His is the noblest profession because in his person he plays out the roles of three other of the noblest professions simultaneously: the soldier, the priest and the artist.

As much as the military a strong and loyal police are the ultimate guardians of the safety of the state and the protectors of its citizens. The soldier protects the country and its people from its external enemies at the cost, if necessary, of his life. The policeman stands in a similar position against the internal enemy. Without the policeman the strongest will always win, the corrupt and crooked will oppress the poor, and the lives, liberties and property of all citizens will be permanently at risk. He, like the soldier, is the first lonely outpost guarding society from its perennial enemies of lawlessness, chaos and men's most violent instincts. Balzac would have equated the policeman with A. E. Housman's mercenary soldier in his weary responsibility and lonely reliability.

The second noblest profession, for Balzac, was that of priest. The priest is a tormented person, living close to evil, a prey to all, and attracting all, temptation. His exposed nerve makes him peculiarly sensitive to guilt, hopelessness and sacrifice. He undertakes his life's work not because he is a kindly, gentle and forgiving soul, but because he is haunted by the harshness, brutality and implacable nature of human life. His premonitions are those of maleficence, of the presence of evil, of the proximity of the unknown. He too is at the frontiers of chaos, but his enemy is the spiritual destroyer within rather than the physical intruder from without. The good priest is closer to the sinner than to the good man. He lives on the margins of society with the wicked man as his constant companion. His vocation is to fight evil, but he is attracted to his vocation by his understanding of evil. He is closer to the rogue in the slums than to the good people on the hill, and he does not deal in comfort but in harsh truths, judgement and punishment. His powers of forgiveness are limited and he can only act vicariously. His right of absolution is not a cheery wave of dismissal, but a benediction upon suffering. His compassion is a bitter acceptance of the vulnerability of men and of the inevitability of suffering and folly.

The policeman and the priest have this in common: an attraction to and a hatred of wrong, a remorseless insistence on guilt and atonement, the exaction of confession, and the hope of remorse and repentance. They both stand in the margins of society, as neither of them gain anything personally by their unrelenting search for the truth of an offence. Both have a sense of moral guardianship, and they follow similar rituals of inquisition, judgement and absolution. They have the same need to identify themselves with what they hate in order to understand it, and they have to distinguish between their repugnance for the act and their understanding of the actor. They are both deeply committed to the darker side of life, its weaknesses, its depravities and its degradation. They both act vicariously, and one does not have to go further than the famous cross-examinations in Simenon, Koestler or le Carré to appreciate the Balzacian parallels.

And it leads the policeman naturally to the noblest profession, so dear to Balzac's heart—that of artist. Both policeman and artist attempt to understand the human condition: to explore motive, to understand the mainspring of action, to enquire into the substance behind the façade. For each the world is the raw material from which to fasten a resemblance to a shadow, and a likeness to an accident. From a jumble of impressions each has to fashion some pattern of order and capture a fleeting moment of truth. The artist, like the policeman, waits for the moment of crisis which may suddenly bring illumination and fix one unique solution from among the welter of inconsequential impressions and glimpses of partial truth. The chameleon nature of the two is well caught in Balzac's master policeman, Vautrin. It is no accident that he is a master of disguise, and that he is above all things an observer. He adapts his protective colouring to his atmosphere and surroundings, and goes unremarked. Like the artist Vautrin is everyman and nobody.

What finally links the policeman to the priest, the soldier and the artist is the instinctive horror all have of chaos, and the professional lives of each are concerned with attempts to fashion some pattern and coherence from the tangled strands of human existence.

This romantic view of police work is too high-flown for Anglo-Saxon tastes but it has important virtues. It affords far more insight into the real nature of police work than does the simple nightwatchman view. The police are involved in society in a unique way, and they are profoundly concerned with some of the most fundamental problems of justice, equity, retribution, punishment, charity and remorse. The policeman who simply reiterates that his role is to apply the law without appreciating the proper significance of what he is saying is at least as great a potential menace as the policeman who consciously thinks of himself as an artist of society, or an avenging priest. The true nature of police work lies somewhere between the extremes of the artisan and the romantic. This can perhaps be more easily seen where the distinction between uniformed and investigating police is more clearly drawn in terms of recruitment and function than it is in common law countries. There is nothing comparable to the French *commissaire de police*, with his triple responsibilities combined with personal independence, in common law police organization.

Both the 'artisanal' and the romantic view of police work have their attendant dangers should a country move into an authoritarian system of government. The workmanlike view of the police encourages those who see in simple violence the panacea for all police problems. Unconcerned with philosophical subtleties the police regard obedience as the highest good; their own obedience to their masters, and the public's obedience to themselves. Unexercised by moral problems the good and the bad fuse into an undifferentiated concept of necessity, and this necessity can be determined by orders from above and order down below.

In these circumstances the police attract to themselves the most dangerous and amoral elements of society—the brutal paranoiacs, the dim-witted sadists, the revengeful social misfits —and because characters of this type perform more efficiently, because more wholeheartedly, the most violent tasks of police work, they become the sergeants and captains of the police system. This process is well documented in the early days of both National Socialist Germany and Soviet Russia. One example can suffice. From the earliest days of the *Cheka* in Russia there were anxious official comments on the internal corruption of the police: 'Reports are coming in from all sides that not only unworthy elements but downright criminals are trying to penetrate the Chekas ... work in the Chekas, conducted in an atmosphere of physical coercion attracts corrupt and downright criminal elements which, profiting from their position as Cheka agents, blackmail and extort, filling their own pockets.'[5] A modern police state requires many policemen, and not simply jealous neighbours, busybodies and street-corner informers. Such a state attracts to the ranks of the police unstable individuals unsuited to authority but envious of it, shifty men who foresee a profitable career, and unwholesome men who relish guilt, pain and the destruction of innocence. They become the workmen of the regime.

The policeman who is the moralist and humanist of the romantic view undergoes different temptations in an authoritarian regime. The prerequisite is that he agree with the principal aims of the regime, and that these are compatible with the soldier-priest-artist concept of the police. A regime which commands respect for its declared intention to protect the state, to eliminate vice, evil, corruption, and to create a new and orderly society out of existing chaos, is likely to establish an initial rapport between itself and its policemen. These are traditional aims, and many people accustomed to the exercise of authority consider them worthy ends.

The policeman, like the civil servant, the judge and the soldier is preconditioned to accept the doctrine of the golden end, the doctrine of the Jesuits, of the *raison d'état*, of the health of the republic, of St Ignatius, of Bismarck and of Gauguin. The policeman like the soldier does not flinch from force, since contact with violence, as well as with human stupidity, is part of his professional life. The danger inherent in this doctrine for the soldier-priest-artist policeman is that, if unchallenged, in the end the soldier may have to sacrifice the women and children, the priest the Jews, and the artist his family.

The process of corruption may not only be easy, it may also be self-induced. The more that demands are made on a policeman's bravery and loyalty, on his understanding of vice and corruption, on his instincts for order and improvement, the more he can lead himself to believe that the police are the only truly moral force in society.

When this moral force is consonant with the moral aims of the regime, and when the regime's moral aims are genuinely consonant with its declared objective morality, little harm comes to the policeman. He is, after all, under no compulsion to be a liberal democrat, a seeker after political truth, or a disciple of Thomas Paine. But if a regime's fine words disguise a more sinister intent, and it knowingly pushes the police apparat into an offensive role in society as its leading instrument for change, the policeman's role changes accordingly. In normal societies the arbitrary nature of police powers is disguised by elaborate social and judicial norms. If the police assume an offensive role, the apparat inevitably resorts to those tactics it understands best: the creation of uncertainty, and the dissemination of fear. The systematic attempt to dominate and lead the public separates the police from the public, and transfers the focus of police loyalties away from society at large to a new internal ethos. The police become forced into the closed conspiracy of a group apart from society, and a new and deformed *esprit de corps* emerges, increased by the police's new sense of public importance, fostered by public cringing, and a new delight in being the possessors of secret powers and secret knowledge.

A regime's deliberate and sustained attempt to harness, for its own unavowed purposes, the policeman's innate desire for order, coherence and form, unhinges the virtue and leaves only the vice. The policeman who was a soldier becomes a hired assassin; he who was a priest becomes a clinical psychologist; and the one who was an artist becomes a predator. And, in the anonymous confines of prison the art of interrogation becomes 'an assault upon identity . . . the establishment of guilt and shame; a form of self-betrayal; alternating leniency and harshness; a compulsion to confess; a final confession, elaborate and inclusive; and emphasis upon the experience of personal rebirth'.[6] The stages are well marked: disorientation, interrogation, rationalization and exploitation.[7] And the policeman can prove, conscienceless, what he has always known: 'There has never been a time since history began when it was not possible, given complete power and lack of scruple, to induce the majority of people to confess to anything, profess or denounce any creed we might wish, and that by the simplest and crudest of methods.'

And the policeman's anger is reserved only for that exception:
'. . . nor has there been, or is ever likely to be, a time when a
stalwart minority will not prefer to resist to the end'.[8]

By then the policeman has lost the virtue of his calling, and
destroyed what he stood, like a legionary, to defend. 'However
honest a man is, however crystal clear his heart, work in the
Chekas which is carried on with almost unlimited rights and
under conditions greatly affecting the nervous system, begins to
tell. Few escape the conditions under which they work.'[9] In the
last stages of the police state the ultimate victims are the police
themselves.

8/The Totalitarian Police State

We have seen that by 1939 Himmler had made Germany into a modern police state. The judiciary was neutralized. The civil service and the army remained as great pillars of the regime but they accepted the police apparat as equal, and recognized its claim to dictate the 'style' of internal administration and to formulate internal government policies. There remained the other great state institution, the National Socialist party. The last phase in the development of the German police state came when the police apparat replaced the party as the ideologues of the state, and transformed the regime into a totalitarian police state.

The National Socialist party differed in several respects from other totalitarian political parties. Its ideology and structure were clearly the antithesis of parties rooted in Marxism-Leninism. It bore some resemblance to Fascist parties in other countries, in that it was nationalistic, élitist, anti-Bolshevik, militaristic, and believed in the virtues of spontaneity, passion, heroism and liberation from conventional bourgeois morality and institutions. All these parties rejected the principles of the French Revolution, believing neither in liberty, equality, fraternity, nor the universal brotherhood of man. But National Socialism differed from more common Fascist doctrine in its emphasis on blood and race, so mystical in its expression and so profound in its reality that it divided the world into three simple camps: the Germanic people and their cousins, who possessed all virtue; other races, so effete, corrupt and decadent that their only role could be to service the master race; and Jews, the deliberate corrupters, polluters, perverters and destroyers of life. The National Socialist conception of the master race claimed for the

Germanic people a unique superiority over all other nations, which were condemned to second-class status. Italian Fascism could rightly claim to be an international doctrine, whose methods, doctrines and the institutions of the corporate state had equal validity in Buenos Aires, Sofia, Budapest, Madrid or Lisbon as in Milan and Rome. National Socialism asserted a unique German supremacy.

It also elevated the Jewish race to a unique position as despoiler of the human race. National Socialist anti-Semitism was not a remnant of perverted Christianity, the jealousy of the market-place, the envy of wealth or the fear of an alien culture, although it played upon all such sentiments. Its anti-Semitism was rooted in primeval instincts and primitive urges; it was not concerned with the secular persecution of Jews in ghettos, street-rioting or social ostracism; it was concerned with the total extermination of the race itself. The Jews were no longer to be the scapegoats of society, they were to be the ultimate sacrifice.

National Socialist tenets denied any aspiration for becoming a universal doctrine. The movement's ideology was also unusual, although not unique, in that it saw the party's role as corporately giving, and demanding, unconditional loyalty to the leader, not only as the source of the party's ideology, but also as the embodiment of the people. The party was the institutionalized expression of the sovereign will, but the party did not claim to be the sovereign; it claimed only to be the vehicle by which that will became reality. This ideology was used to hypnotize the German people with the theories derived from Hitler's Weltanschauung. With its emphasis on the values of spontaneity, of mystical participation in the life of the state, of the virtues of initiative, of trust, of unpremeditated valour in all things, the party had a degree of innate combustion which hardly suited the staider forms of administrative and constitutional law. It was not supposed to; its function was to establish the absolute authority of the Führer as the incarnation of the spirit of the German people, the charismatic leader who drew his inspiration and instincts from the people, the soil and German blood.

It is clear that with such a philosophy there could be no conception of a corporate leadership. All the evidence shows that Hitler's daemon was his own, and could only be touched but never directed. The internal politics of the party therefore became a struggle for Hitler's ear. Himmler's fight with the party would have been a great deal harder had there been a corporate leadership in which personal jockeying for position might have led to genuine political alliances putting in jeopardy the personal administrative empire of any one leader. So long as Hitler drew his reserve powers from his role as Führer, Himmler was in a position of great strength. In a party with a charismatic leader, political opposition within the party apparat becomes personal treason. And the discovery and destruction of traitors is work for the police.

When the Reichssicherheitshauptamt (RSHA) was created in 1939 it took over the party's security organization, the Sicherheitsdienst (SD), and acquired the last great archive of police files and intelligence from the party apparat. It put the party itself under the surveillance of the police, as the normal police were under the direction of the Gestapo, the Gestapo under Heydrich, Heydrich under Himmler. This takeover was moreover promptly emphasized by the practice that grew up in the early days of the war of amalgamating party office with police office at the higher levels of police administration. The office thus created was that of *Höhere-SS-und-Polizeiführer*, and many of Himmler's 'special' tasks were entrusted to these officers during the war, in particular on the Eastern front.

The takeover had immediate effects. Heydrich's report of July 2, 1940, on the invasion of Poland, showed the reality of the new power structure *vis-à-vis* the army.

> Co-operation with the troops below staff level and in many cases with the various army staffs was in general good. On the other hand, in many cases the more senior

army commanders adopted a fundamentally different approach to the basic problems of suppression of the enemies of the State. This approach, primarily due to ignorance of the strength of the ideological opposition, gave rise to friction and counter-orders contravening the political activity undertaken by the Reichsführer-SS in accordance with the instructions of the Führer. . . . The reason was that the directives governing police activity were exceptionally far reaching—for instance, the liquidation of numerous Polish leading circles running into thousands of persons was ordered. Such an order could not be divulged to the general run of military headquarters, still less to members of the staffs. To the uninitiated therefore the action of the Police and the SS appears arbitrary, brutal, and unauthorised.[1]

But Heydrich did not doubt that the police were the authorities, and were carrying out the only will they recognized, the will of the Führer. The army was trapped by Himmler in a web, its own trap of military justice. It was made into a conspiratorial body in a way which would have rendered troops liable to court-martial if they disobeyed. The 'General Instructions for the Treatment of Political Commissars', promulgated on June 6, 1941 for the Russian campaign, were issued to a restricted group of the most senior officers, with explicit instructions that the consequential orders must be conveyed by word of mouth. The orders were given a gloss to explain the necessity for handing over Russian political commissars to Himmler's extermination units, when 'regard for justice must in certain circumstances give place to military necessity', and it was (unfortunately) sometimes necessary to revert to 'the ancient usages of war'. This was language which soldiers could use and understand, though it was not Himmler's natural language; but he learned it well enough to quieten the consciences of the soldiers, while obtaining and demonstrating the reality of power.

In August 1943 Himmler was appointed minister of the interior, and the pattern was complete. The totalitarian police state had been fully achieved. Himmler's dream of 1939—that the police should be the sole instrument of the political will of the Führer—had come to pass. The police were no longer considered a normal part of the state administration; they had an 'overall political mission' which required no legal backing for such individual measures as might be demanded. The police apparat was responsible for political direction and was the institution for the execution of the Führer's will. It was the incarnation of the mobilization system, of political development and of social initiative.

The police apparat had consolidated its supreme position. Its general effect on society can be illustrated by a personal memorandum from Hans Frank, former minister of justice in Bavaria, governor general of Poland, staunch party member:

> Unfortunately the view appears to be growing, even among leading National Socialists, that the greater the uncertainty regarding the legal position of the ordinary citizen, the more secure is the position of the authorities. Arbitrary use of police executive power is now so general that it is not too much to say that the individual citizen has lost all rights in law. This situation can, of course, be justified by the necessity to concentrate all national energies upon a single aim and to ensure that opposition factions have no opportunity to interfere with the course of the popular liberation programme. . . . As things are today, when any citizen can be consigned to a concentration camp for any length of time without any possibility of redress, when there is no longer any security of life, freedom, honour, or honestly earned possessions, it is my firm conviction that any ethical relationship between the leadership of the State and its citizens is being totally destroyed.[2]

This was the reality of the totalitarian police state. And when, in 1944, the army in the last resort came to challenge the power of the Führer, no longer by open means but by conspiracy, Himmler achieved the final decision. The army found too late that his SS was not only the police, in the contemptuous way soldiers refer to the police: it was also an important military force in its own right. The police apparat's élite force, the Waffen-SS, provided Himmler with his ace. In the last resort the civil service had been beaten by the force of regulations, the army by the force of arms. The police were in supreme control. They were better ideologues than the party, better soldiers than the army, better administrators than the civil service, and better executioners than the judges.

We can now begin to provide a formal explanation of this process. Ionescu defines a totalitarian regime as having the following characteristics: a compulsory ideology, a monolithic party, a monopoly of communications, a monopoly of all means of armed combat, a centrally directed economy and a terrorist political police. We can therefore say that all totalitarian regimes are authoritarian, but not all authoritarian regimes are totalitarian. Thus an authoritarian regime may have a free enterprise economic system, or an official religion without a compulsory ideology, or it may rely upon military controls rather than on a political police. An authoritarian regime may allow only one political party, but that may be justified simply on grounds of political efficiency or economic development. Alternatively only members of the party may be expected to accept the party's political philosophy, and that philosophy may have no transcendental pretensions.

But one of the characteristic features of a totalitarian ideology is that it claims to know the laws of world history and to afford a unique insight into their proper use. It also lays claim to a body of revealed truths which industrious and intelligent men of good will must find self-evident. This ideology rapidly produces an argument in which good and evil, right and wrong, as judged by normal standards, are superseded concepts. With totalitarian ideologies 'the law of progress can be divorced from normal values and presented as a law of nature'.[3]

In totalitarian states the party is both the arena in which the ideology is worked out and the guardian of that ideology. It is within the party that the passionate debates on doctrine and the true meaning of the revealed world take place. Ideologies show marked similarities to medieval religions in which the world is divided into the elect who have received the doctrine, the initiates who are prepared to receive the doctrine, the people who are to be saved, the unbeliever who might be cured, and the infidel who is an offence against the light and holy truth. This becomes, in modern terminology, the members of the central committee, the candidate members, the mass of the people, the potential opposition and the enemies of the people.

The party is the custodian of the revealed truth and the formulator of policy. The party inevitably comes to view its opponents as not only wrong in practical political judgements, but also as morally heinous. Errors cannot be rectified by rational argument and explanation; they can only be purged by expiation. Opposition is then not simply a form of error, but a rejection of the good.

Lenin himself had doubts as to the wisdom of giving the party constitutional authority as the supreme arbiter of political power. He feared that, since doctrine was likely to be evolutionary, constitutional authority would weaken the party as a revolutionary instrument. The curious result of this reasoning was that the revolutionary police in Russia, regarded as the defensive organ of the revolutionary state, obtained prior recognition as a leading state authority. The justification: 'The State is a sphere of coercion. It would be madness to renounce coercion especially in the epoch of the dictatorship of the proletariat; an administrative approach and "steerage" are indispensable.'[4] In practice, the party in Russia did become the dominant

apparat for a time, and party members were appointed to leading positions in all the other state apparats to ensure conformity
to the party's directives. In the totalitarian state a compulsory
ideology is imposed upon the purposes and functioning of normal
constitutional and administrative institutions.

The realm of control, however, increasingly expands as overt
obedience to the party's directives is reinforced by attempts to
ensure genuine compliance of outlook. Hence the importance of
thought control and internal propaganda. Alleged intentions
can then become the basis of treason, and ideological heresy is a
sin marking a man as an enemy of the people. The belief in a
mission is of overriding importance, and with it comes the passionate desire to ensure right thinking in all the subordinate
parts of the state. Hume put it very well: 'It is on opinion only
that government is founded; and the maxim extends to the most
despotic and most military governments, as well as the most free
and popular. The Soldan of Egypt or the Emperor of Rome
might drive his subjects like brute beasts against their sentiments
and inclinations; but he must, at least, have led his Mamelukes
or Praetorian bands, like men, by their opinions.'[5]

The greatest crime that can be committed in a totalitarian
state is for members of the party to become ideologically corrupt.
Their crime is the crime of the cardinal, not the offence of the
unbeliever. Not only do they betray the faith, they endanger the
state and subvert the people. The party is always the most sensitive apparat in the totalitarian state since it claims leadership
and the control of other apparatus, and it alone controls and
purges its own membership. In the totalitarian state the party is
self-operating in a unique way.

But should the party itself fall under suspicion, and its probity
and integrity be called into question, the terror which has been
administered on behalf of the party will be turned against it. The
totalitarian state becomes a totalitarian police state.

The powers of the police are always proportionate to the
authoritarianism of the regime. When that authoritarianism is

reinforced by a compulsory ideology and a monopolistic political party a totalitarian state is formed. While the party remains dominant the police have their authority as a leading state body, but the police remain subject to the over-all control of the party. When the party is undermined, the way is open for the police to move up to become the leading apparat of the state, assuming the party's role of ultimate guardian of ideological purity. The police apparat takes on itself the responsibility for mobilizing society, but, with the intellectual limitations of the police, the weapon most likely to be used is terror, and the terror, in the first instance, is turned against the party. In Hitler's Germany, as in Stalin's Russia, one can trace the purges of the old guard of the party, the cowing of other apparats, and by progressive stages the massive expansion of forced labour, concentration camps, mass murders and deportations. As Ionescu plainly puts it: 'The weapons of terror are then used not principally as a means of collective punishment, but as the means by which the primitive main apparat (now the Police) attempts to undertake in terrible caricature the functions of social and economic mobilisation of the apparat as a whole.'[6]

The police apparat then comes to regard itself as the only wholly reliable bastion of the state, and to consider all other apparats as suspect. The professional scepticism of policemen becomes elevated to a theory of the state. In a totalitarian state the party, with its knowledge of doctrine, can distinguish good from bad, right from wrong, correct from false views, and the good citizen from the enemy of the people. In a totalitarian police state all is suspect, everyone a potential traitor. While the party rules it is possible to lead the good life by following the precepts of guided conscience, intellectual humility and personal probity. In the totalitarian police state none of this is a safeguard, for all might hide an even deeper treachery, and disguise the most determined and plausible villain.

In this vacuum the police apparat picks up the form and words of the ideology, but, because of its inherent limitations, translates them into simple, bureaucratic, regulatory police measures which it can understand. The result is a distorted mirror with the dynamism and creativeness which might have belonged to the party being reduced to a static Euclidean model of government. The country is left with the arbitrary implementation of laws which are no more than police regulations, which the police themselves do not undertake to observe, and principles which are no more than tenuous guides to safe conduct. 'The clumsy attempts of the police personnel, with police conceptions and methods, to run the entire state machine, transforms the State into endless labour camps, brigades of inmate-citizens, and barracks of mass education.'[7] In attaining a position beyond their capacity to comprehend, the police become instruments of their own misconceptions, the victims of their own apprehensions, and destroyers of all that the police stand for: law, morality, justice and safety.

9/Conclusion

To conclude this study we should consider the place of the police state in the contemporary world, and its likely future as a system of government. As we shall see both the traditional police state and the totalitarian police state seem to have good chances of surviving for fairly lengthy periods of time. The modern police state appears to be intrinsically more vulnerable. It is also important in this summing-up very briefly to consider some of the features for which a political scientist should look when analysing systems of government in the terms of our previous discussion. It would also be unrealistic to close without some passing reference to the philosophical and political foundations upon which a police state is built.

We look first at the three types of police state in their contemporary setting. The traditional police state was a mixture of autocratic reform, modernization, benevolence, suspicion and compulsion. The system of government invented by the Cameralists quite easily accords with the concepts of national development held in many so-called third-world countries today. But, as Joseph II found, not only may the integrity, loyalty and instinctive dynamism of public officials be open to doubt, their ideological loyalty may also be in question. This is as readily explicable today as it was in the eighteenth century. Rapid development is conditional on breaking up established political and economic relationships. Passive resistance is always possible and it may be deliberately fostered by questioning the legitimacy of the regime itself. Leaders convinced of the ultimate benefits that will be gained for their country are always likely to be tempted to overcome inertia or resistance to their programme by resorting to coercion and strict regulation.

In terms of power, although not necessarily in terms of money, the civil service is, generally, the first beneficiary of rapid development. Two hundred years have shown that if it is properly organized and stimulated it can become the framework of the state, promoting, guiding and mobilizing society. Very few countries these days place their confidence in natural laws of economics, and see in bureaucracy the instrument-elect for enforced growth. General police powers are increased to ensure compliance with social and economic plans, and these powers are concentrated to provide the 'steerage' which Lenin mentioned. With an honest civil service and upright leaders the police then become the workmen of the regime, regulating the traffic of day-to-day ordinances, and applying general policing regulations to individual cases.

If, however, experience shows a country's leaders (or leader) that there is reason to lack confidence in the integrity and loyalty of the civil service they will institute a system of secret checks to ensure obedience, enforce honesty and to apply sanctions. Furthermore, if the same leaders regard public opinion as immature and too malleable (which may simply mean that they fear opposition), they will resort to Fouché's tactics and infiltrate all potential opposition movements in order to teach the virtues of co-operation and the disadvantages of resistance. In both these cases the powers of the police services will be increased, and from being a subordinate instrument of the bureaucracy these services will become an apparat in their own right. It may further be observed that should the leaders as well as the civil service be corrupt and inept, the police will be powerless, and likely to turn, like the rest of the population, to the army as the saviour of last resort.

The traditional police state, then, is an organized state, devoted to mobilization and development, with extensive police powers concentrated in a civil service under a single political directing will, with a police apparat enjoying a national watching brief over the safety of the state, the integrity of public officers and the morale of the population.

The modern police state takes all this several stages further. It, too, presupposes an authoritarian regime, but in modern terms, not the terms of the Enlightenment. It has to come to terms with the effects of a century of theorizing about the nature of democracy, the formation of political parties, the effects of mass media, and the complexity of modern economics and mass education. An authoritarian regime now involves creating a system in which the executive branch of government dominates the legislature and the judiciary; in which by various devices the electorate has either been tamed or cowed; in which freedom of expression is limited by boundaries set unilaterally at the discretion of the executive; in which organized interest groups are controlled, through, for example, official trade unions, or controlled trade associations; in which public policy is formulated in circles neither responsible nor necessarily responsive to public opinion; in which public opinion is consciously moulded by government controlled agencies.

The nature of an authoritarian regime is determined by the balance of forces within the system. The police apparat is normally a subordinate branch of government acting as enforcer of the executive's will. The first stage in the development of a modern police state is the centralization of all police services, if hitherto they have been on a local footing, or have been divided between different national administrations. The second stage is when the police apparat becomes dominated internally by the political police force, and the interests and procedures of the uniformed and criminal police services become subordinated to the special needs, functions and operational requirements of the political police.

This is followed by an encroachment by the police apparat, under one pretext or another, on the general police powers of other state institutions, and in particular those of the civil service for licensing, inspecting and controlling trade, the professions, education, the communications media, social security agencies, and government agencies with overseas interests. This encroachment is matched by inroads into the judicial domain, the police apparat obtaining powers of arrest, supervision and detention, and a right to inflict penal sanctions outside the control of the normal judicial machinery.

Finally, the police apparat detaches itself from its dependence on the army for armed force, and either a riot police section is reinforced with armoured vehicles or a standing gendarmerie becomes a para-military force subordinate to the police authorities. When the police apparat is immune to control by the civil service, the judiciary and the army, and is an independent leading state institution in its own right, a modern police state has been formed.

In a totalitarian police state different issues arise. In the normal totalitarian state the party is corporately the custodian of the ideology, and the police apparat remains a subordinate part of the system, on a par with the civil service, the judiciary and the army. The party has a monopoly of political direction. But if this monopoly is instead regarded as the perquisite of one charismatic leader, as it was in Hitler's Germany, the party itself is a subordinate part of the system of government, primarily responsible for invigorating the population and for providing explanatory glosses for the leader's decisions. In these circumstances, the police apparat has to dislodge the party from any special relationship with the leader. When the police apparat replaces the party in a totalitarian state as the custodian of the ideology and the prime political mover, a totalitarian police state is formed. This is the culmination of a process which started two hundred years ago. It completes on the one hand a cycle of administrative history which its founders could never have envisaged; and, on the other, a way of thinking about politics which has its intellectual origins in the work of passionate and idealistic reformers.

The historical evidence we have suggests that the traditional police state can be a very stable form of government, lasting for several decades, provided that the legitimacy of the ruler is recognized. It seems to outgrow itself by its very success in reforming the structure of society. The attacks upon it come from those offended by its authoritarianism rather than by its administrative structure. Throughout the nineteenth century liberal reformers were concerned with the concentration of power, attempting to bring under more popular control the policy-making elements of government. Little was heard of any demands for administrative reform; indeed, most jurists and publicists were more concerned with improving the quality of the existing administrative services than with remodelling them. New leaders of reformed states simply demanded that these services transfer their loyalties to the new regime rather than change their concepts of what was appropriate to police administration.

There is some evidence to suggest that totalitarian police states can also last for fairly long periods. We should add pre-1945 Japan to the examples of Hitler's Germany and Stalin's Russia which we have already cited. It is clear that in Japan the police apparat had a similar position as guardian of the ideology —if we equate a compulsory state religion with a political ideology. The apparat enforced the broadly drafted police regulations and orders governing the internal life of the country, paying particular attention to 'thought control', and to stamping out dissent, which it equated with internal subversion. Its board of 'Shrines' (*Jingiin*) controlled state Shinto, which was the institutional expression of the cult of the emperor, and through a system of administrative jurisdictions it effectively restricted the independence of the judiciary.[1]

In all three countries the system seems to have worked in terms of the mobilization of the nation, of economic development and of national self-discipline. It is very striking that their enemies were continually impressed by the loyalty of their citizens to the regime, if the best test for this is found in a passionate defence of one's country. The evidence, indeed, suggests that the totalitarian state rather than the totalitarian police state is more subject to internal pressures and resistance. The examples we have show numerous instances within totalitarian regimes of the growth of institutional rivalries and threats of internal scission. Factions become the nearest substitute for political groups, damaging the internal cohesion of the main state institutions. In the totalitarian state economic and social pluralism is always present to threaten the somewhat artificial unity imposed by the party.[2] But within the totalitarian police state it seems that the police apparat, by freezing the ideology into a caricature of itself, and emptying it of its dynamism and creativity, does succeed in enforcing a genuine conformity of thought and political aspiration.

This is not surprising. When the policeman turns psychologist, assassin and predator he combines in himself some of the more maleficent arts, and these he uses for the subtler forms of terror. The open terror of violence on the streets and in the cells, brought against the opponents of the regime, is gradually replaced by the silent terror of coercing citizens to collaborate. That is, the police apparat comes to see that its long-term aim must be not to destroy enemies of the regime, but to prevent their emergence. It impresses the policeman's view of the good man on society—which is simply that the good man obeys the law, causes no trouble and does not resist. This then opens up whole fields of education, indoctrination, rehabilitation, self-improvement and the creation of new personalities. The instruments of overt violence are supplemented by the subtler tools of persuasion. If the entire apparatus of the state is used by the police apparat to create its version of the model citizen, a genuinely new man emerges, conditioned to compliance, conformity and voluntary obedience.

The modern police state, on the other hand, seems to be an intrinsically unstable form of government. It rarely lasts more than four or five years, whereas other forms of authoritarian regime seem to be able to last indefinitely in favourable circumstances. The modern police state's vulnerability appears to lie in the very nature of its operations.

In the first instance, the centralization of police services on which it is founded breeds plain inefficiency. Most administrative studies show that beyond a certain point centralization is counter-productive, and the quality of service declines with a dilution in the quality of personnel employed. This counter-productivity can be especially marked in the case of the police service since the efficiency of the service depends on two things: the collection of reliable information and the use of force. Force, however, is useless, and may be self-defeating if it is not guided by good intelligence.

Police intelligence in all systems relies essentially upon an organized network of informers. There are voluntary informers and impressed informers. Both types are intrinsically suspect. Voluntary informers may be inspired by personal motives of greed, hatred or ideology. Such men are to be found in all levels of society, from embassies to bars. But the voluntary nature of their work makes their information doubtful until a long record of accuracy has been established. The number of useful voluntary informers is strictly limited. The establishment of a police state, however, increases the number of volunteers, many of whom seize the opportunity to pay off old scores or to ingratiate themselves with the new masters. The result is that intelligence becomes suspect as ancient rancours, petty gossip and malicious rumour begin to take the place of authentic political intelligence.

Impressed informers from this point of view are more reliable. They are generally recruited from people who are on the fringe of criminal or subversive activities, and they may already be open to formal charges. Their co-operation is forced by bribes and threats, and they are always in a dilemma: not only may the police denounce them to the courts, they may also denounce them to their associates, which carries a consequent risk to their professional futures. Other impressed informers come from the ranks of those whose livelihoods are in the hands of the police.

The power to license a trade can have very important results, and, of course, every police force tolerates businesses outside the law in order to ensure co-operation when it is needed, and to concentrate criminal elements in a restricted number of haunts. The impressed informer tends, however, to be inadequate as his primary concern is to provide accurate factual information which can be tested by the police without involving himself. He rarely volunteers information of genuine political importance since this requires sophisticated reporting of attitudes and not simply the cataloguing of events.

A police system which comes to rely upon these two sources for its information finds that good intelligence becomes lost in a swamp of trivia, and reliable officials become overburdened with the control of unreliable agents. The only wholly satisfactory way for a political police apparat in a police state to operate is for it to create its own opportunities. In the long term it has to infiltrate its own agents into genuinely critical areas of social and political life. This takes time; infiltration which does not arouse suspicions requires a fairly lengthy period of passivity on the part of an agent and his gradual absorption into a group. In the short term the political police have most success in identifying dissidents by the creation of secret resistance groups under police control. The establishment of an underground network enables the political police not only to identify dissidents at an early stage, but also to manipulate the politics of the underground into an approved direction. It may also be used to incriminate members of other state institutions if this suits the political purposes of the police.

The general tendency of the police apparat in a police state is for it to attempt to control every field open to infiltration. The deliberate restriction of its activities to genuinely critical areas of enquiry seems to be too sophisticated a policy to be generally followed. Police intelligence becomes an end in itself, since there are always good police reasons for knowing as much as possible about everyone, and it is apparently operationally desirable to be able to intervene promptly at all stages. But the police apparat is operationally handicapped if in practice it genuinely attempts to be ubiquitous rather than being content simply to create that impression. The operations of the RSHA during the war establish this point very clearly. In attempting to be cognizant of every rumour and current of opinion, and simultaneously to transmit the orders of Himmler across the continent, severe bureaucratic confusion was created. On grounds of secrecy, police intelligence was kept separate from the executive branches, and there were many cases of gross inefficiency arising out of this. Furthermore, the machine became so swamped with undifferentiated intelligence that by the time the information had been processed into manageable summaries it had lost its living pertinence and was largely a morass of irrelevancies. On the other hand, it is clear that when the German counter-intelligence organizations worked with economy of effort and personnel they were highly successful in penetrating and misleading underground resistance groups. In many ways the history of the Special Operations Executive in Europe is as much a testimonial to the exceptional skill, daring and inventiveness of German counter-espionage departments, as it is a memorial to the heroism of SOE's own agents.

The fascination with collecting intelligence for its own sake brings the police apparat into conflict with the other state institutions. Its search for information leads it to demand access to the documents of all other public authorities, to undertake surveillance of mail, publications, and radio and television networks, and to make overt as well as secret enquiries into the personal affairs of politicians, civil servants, journalists and army officers. This distrust and suspicion, on which the power of the political police depends, can easily turn against the police apparat as a whole. The police in a modern police state are not the only state institution interested in obtaining intelligence or in purveying news or suppressing or distorting information. They may well be in competition with the party, the army intelligence services, or with trained bureaucratic specialists in the ministries. The attempt by the police to control communications inevitably brings them into conflict with the other great state institutions.

The vulnerability of the police apparat in a modern police state stems from its involvement in politics, the very essence of its power. Police forces tend to be professionally orientated towards a defensive role in society, and when they assume an offensive role they have to deal with the professionals of politics, the civil servants, the generals and the politicians themselves. A police apparat in an offensive role is inevitably identified with the principal leaders of the regime. When the authority of the leaders declines through mismanagement, corruption or intrigue, the police apparat has a comparable fall from grace. It can easily become the scapegoat of a regime. In this respect it has neither the amorphous anonymity of the civil service, nor the apparent independence of the judiciary, nor the natural authority of the army. Under pressure the police apparat itself can disintegrate, leaving the political police branch isolated. The bluff workman-like sections of uniformed police are easily persuaded that as a uniformed force in the public eye they have more in common with the other armed services than with the intrigues and spying of the backrooms. An alliance between the uniformed police and the army against the leader and the political police branch led to the overthrow of Nkrumah in Ghana. And in times of stress members of a police administration may instinctively demonstrate allegiance to other bureaucrats in the civil service rather than to their official superiors in the police service.

In the last resort a police apparat is vulnerable because its leaders are always dispensable and can be replaced by officials from other state institutions. It is never regarded as prima facie strange for a police service to be headed by an administrator, a colonel or a man of law. The professionalism of a policeman, when put to the test, is less than that of members of the other great state institutions; or, better, the kind of professionalism a policeman has is politically more easily dispensed with than that of other officials. A police apparat seems destined to be either an instrument or a master, and to maintain its position of first among equals in a modern police state it always requires some allies among members of other state institutions. But the very nature of its work and its methods of operations antagonize other groups, and it can easily become the object of the vagaries of administrative politics which mark authoritarian regimes.

This study has involved an analysis of the recent institutional histories of the following countries: Albania, Yugoslavia, Argentina, Brazil, Portugal, Spain, Czechoslovakia, Syria, Iraq, Egypt, Algeria, Cuba, Greece, the German Democratic Republic, Ghana, Indonesia, the U.S.S.R., China, Japan, Italy and France. Not all these countries have had police state regimes in the recent past, but they all have powerful police services which are interesting to look at simply for comparative purposes. I have been mainly concerned in the latter part of the study with building an abstract model of the different types of police state. This has the disadvantages of all model-building exercises, but nevertheless seemed to be the wisest course to follow in this case. If the concept of 'the police state' is to be of any value to political science the term must first be shorn of its wholly pejorative sense of simple political abuse. But since it still possesses these overtones I have wished to avoid becoming entangled in a wrangling match with people of passionate convictions who consider too aloof a study of politics inhuman and amoral. Futhermore, since, as I have insisted, a police state is only one form of authoritarian regime, and may be a fairly unstable type at that, I have no wish to stigmatize one particular country at the time of writing for a form of government which might well have been changed by the time of publication.

With this proviso, I will offer some indications of what a political scientist looks for if he wishes to make the concept of the police state operational. The reports of journalists and travellers, as well as studies by professional scholars, often provide valuable starting points.

In Yugoslavia in 1966 rumours circulated widely that the police apparat was beginning to threaten the supremacy of the party, and to infiltrate its agents into leading positions in other state institutions. The party reacted quickly and instituted a massive enquiry, and a plenary meeting of the Central Committee was called. Two senior members of the party were charged with obstructing the party line on economic and social affairs, and with encouraging the secret police to enquire into party affairs and the management of public business. The offending members were stripped of their police functions and replaced. The scale of the effort made by the police apparat to become the dominant political force can be judged by the ensuing purge in which several hundred employees of the ministry were removed from office, and the number of officials employed in the security services was halved. An abortive attempt to establish the necessary preconditions for a police state.[3]

Recent accounts of purges and public executions in Iraq have features which should be noted. The Ba'athist Party's manifesto when it came to power said that 'the security apparatus is one of the agencies which must be placed in the direct hands of the party without reservations';[4] and the party's own security apparatus, which at one time formed the backbone of the National Guard, an ill-organized militia, has come to dominate the regular police services, and assumed the functions of a secret political police. It has infiltrated the army, and has attacked senior officials and service officers known to be close to the president. This new political police has also come to dominate the party itself, and has displaced the officers of the regular security forces who had a reputation for being traditionally non-political.

An almost classic description of the totalitarian police state is contained in a report on Albania by a most distinguished journalist. Albania has a compulsory ideology and a monolithic party. In addition there is complete direction of labour, all foreign contacts are forbidden, the press is censored, and jobs, homes and holidays are dependent upon having a clean record with the secret police. The party itself is infiltrated with police agents and its members kept under strict surveillance by the police apparat. The police comprise a substantial force, and control parts of the civil service and the defence forces. The police employ large numbers of informers, and have trained children systematically to report anything that they see or hear at home or in the streets which is critical of President Hoxha or Chairman Mao.[5]

Small items of news may be significant in indicating the internal movement of forces within a regime. The General Law Amendment Act of June 30, 1969, in South Africa made a Bureau of State Security exempt from public scrutiny, and gave the state, on production of a certificate by a cabinet minister or authorized officials, powers to prohibit the hearing of evidence in court if it is deemed prejudicial to the state, and could overrule the courts on the admissibility of other evidence.[6] On the other hand, in West Pakistan the High Court ruled that even under the emergency regulations of martial law an individual must always have the right of appeal in spite of arbitrary regulations. The judgement is worth quoting:

> We have no cavil with the proposition of law that no martial law regulation can, or order could, be challenged in this court, but it must be remembered that there is nothing in the provisional constitution order or martial law regulations which bars the superior courts of this country from interpreting the martial law regulations. No one, including the chief martial law administrator, can transcend or deviate from the sole purpose of restoring law and order and democracy, and it needs no gainsaying that the curbing of the jurisdiction of the established judiciary is not a step in that direction and it

is for this reason that the chief martial law administrator never made any secret of that fact.[7]

Or, again, in Portugal, the prime minister has publicly stated that 'the police must be an instrument of the state, and not a super-state, and must act within legal limits and not be exorbitant'. This was followed shortly afterwards by the abolition of the political police, the PIDE, as a separate force, and its amalgamation into the Directorate General of Security within the Ministry of the Interior where it would be under stricter administrative control.[8]

The post-war history of Czechoslovakia could well be taken as a model of a regime passing from a liberal democracy, to a modern police state, to a totalitarian state, to a totalitarian police state, to an interregnum; and now, more recently, to a reversal of policy, under foreign compulsion, to a new authoritarian regime whose emerging characteristics suggest at the minimum a modern police state, with the possibility of development once again to a full-fledged totalitarian police state.

We end with an example in which we will consider the internal development of a country which has had all the potential for developing into a modern police state, but which until now has not done so, remaining a plain military autocracy.

In April 1967 a military junta took over the government of Greece in a *coup d'état*. The government it displaced could loosely be termed a liberal democracy with a strong monarchical executive. This system of government had been created after a good deal of fratricidal strife at the end of the war in which Communist-led partisans had been guilty of some disgraceful crimes against the common law, as well as engaging in the more 'normal' partisan activities which were common in Europe at that time. As a result of this civil war the new liberal regime maintained a system of police surveillance over the political life of the country not altogether consonant with the doctrines of the purest liberalism: comprehensive police files on political suspects were kept; there were political prisoners and exiles; certificates of social beliefs were demanded; special legislation gave the government extensive powers of search and arrest. The new system of government also inherited a tradition of personal and party politics which led to a considerable degree of instability, although this was to some extent counter-balanced by a well trained army, loyalist and monarchical in its tradition. The *coup d'état* was led by senior officers who held that the existing parliamentary system had so corrupted the life of the country that revolutionary forces threatened to take over.

From the earliest days of the new regime acute observers were concerned at the likelihood that Greece would rapidly evolve into a modern police state. Thus reporters from *The Times* made a detailed examination of the conditions in Greece after four months of the regime's existence. They concluded that military rule might last a long time, and that therefore it was important

> . . . that the habits and vocabulary of the police state should not emerge in these early days and harden into principles of government. The omens are uncomfortable. An opponent of the regime is missing; the Government prevaricates over his fate; . . . meanwhile all over Greece extraordinary courts-martial grind out extraordinary sentences; and behind the unchanged face of tourist Greece that power of the Asphalia, or C.I.D., grows remorselessly. . . . Well over 100 Greeks have been arrested for purely political crimes. These include insulting the Army, the flag, the Government, the King, the Queen . . . spreading false reports, indulging in revolutionary proselytism, painting 'communist' slogans on walls, singing communist songs, disobeying a command of the military authority, and harbouring wanted persons without declaring them to the police. Some of these activities were crimes before the coup, but no one in Greece pretends the scale of repression is unchanged.

Over 80 people have been sentenced by extraordinary courts-martial, usually to terms of imprisonment. . . . No doubt that one vote cast for the communists was sufficient grounds for deportation. Those without such records can be held for up to a week without charge. And the court martial which hears the charge—as confirmed by the Defence Minister—admits of no appeal.

The most sinister aspect of these new dispensations is the enormous power given to the security authorities. In practice this usually devolves on the Asphalia, which literally means 'security'; this civilian body operates very much like an English police force's C.I.D. It can also act on behalf of the military intelligence authorities. . . . Informers are suspected of being everywhere. There are stories of waiters ringing up Asphalia reporting conversations at their table, of taxi drivers driving straight to Asphalia with talkative customers. . . . The regime has admitted that telephones are being cut off; the reason offered is that it prevents left wing elements from plotting over the phone. The Government has made it an offence to criticise the regime over the telephone. There are two documented cases of the police taking action against such offenders.[9]

Reports from other reliable and responsible sources were much the same. The *Sunday Telegraph* of November 12, 1967, reported that parliament was closed down, the constitution suspended and political parties proscribed. It continued:

The Press has been gagged, most youth organisations disbanded, trade unions brought under government control, the civil service purged, mayors and local officials dismissed, and strict censorship imposed on radio, films and theatre. . . . Telephones are tapped, private mail perused, idle conversations reported to the police by numerous informers, and any overt displays of criticism severely punished. Not only are potential leaders of an organised opposition being locked up, but virtually anyone who spreads what the regime calls 'malicious lies'. ... [but] drastic as its methods have been, the junta has garnered a good deal of sympathy among ordinary Greeks. Bureaucratic inefficiency, widespread nepotism, and a paralysing corruption in virtually every area of public life had sapped public confidence in the old regime.

From these reports certain features stand out: the establishment of an authoritarian regime as we have described it in an earlier chapter; the transformation of the criminal police into a political police; the expansion of the political police into a body used for the control of opinion; the development of all the apparatus for permanent surveillance of the population through widespread networks of informers and the control of communications; the substitution for the judiciary of extraordinary courts, though these are still under military control; extensive powers of arrest and preventive detention based on emergency powers and the application of numerous laws of exception.

Since the end of the first year of the regime the three principal apparats of the state have been attacked, and systematic police action has created an atmosphere of anxiety and uncertainty. There have been numerous arrests for resistance activities, and over 100 bomb explosions in Athens. What is striking is the number of resistance groups uncovered, and the speed with which this has been accomplished. The normal pattern of political police activity would suggest that a certain number of these groups have police origins, as, if true to form, would some of the bomb explosions. The Greek political police have a long and sophisticated history, and a subtlety that clearly defeated *The Times* reporter who innocently accepted the story that telephones were being cut off to prevent seditious gossip and underground plotting. Since the interception of communications is one of the principal weapons in the situation that was described, it is inconceivable that any trained political police force would destroy so valuable a source of intelligence.

The civil service was the first apparat to be attacked, as clearly, from the *Sunday Telegraph's* report, it was the most vulnerable to the charges of corruption and inefficiency. The Act of August 29, 1967 permitted the suspension or dismissal of permanent civil servants if they had been guilty of immorality or conduct prejudicial to the service; if they had been negligent in, or incapable of, performing their duties; if they had failed to carry out their duties properly because of malice or personal interest; if they lacked the necessary moral standing; if they had actively campaigned for a political party or given or obtained favours for political reasons. The disciplinary tribunal consisted of a permanent director or secretary of the ministry, a judge and a senior military officer; permanent civil servants dismissed, after confirmation by the minister, had no further right of appeal, and received a month's salary in lieu of notice.

The actions against the civil service led indirectly to the attack on the judiciary. Several senior legal officials were removed from office under this act, and appealed against their dismissal to the Greek Council of State. The council insisted on its right to be heard, and issued a judgement reinstating twenty-one of the officials.[10] The president of the council was immediately suspended, and his resignation—which had never been offered —was accepted. Nine other judges on the council promptly resigned in sympathy. One of the leading officials whom the council had reinstated, and three of the prominent lawyers who had defended him and his colleagues, were arrested by the police and deported to remote mountain villages.

The army in its turn fell under police surveillance. Reports from various sources have noted that a large number of senior officers have been either prematurely retired or arrested and exiled on charges of royalist sympathies. In many of these cases the officers were sympathetic to the regime when it first took power, but later lost faith in its performance. Other reports have noted a significant number of former officers involved in resistance activities, and many popular officers have been followed by security police as a matter of routine, and been detained and exiled.[11]

There is also evidence that torture has been used as an administrative instrument by the police authorities and the case has been strengthened by the publication of the report of the European Human Rights Commission. Numerous other reports testify to a sense of the ubiquity of informers and the political police. Here, again, we can see the familiar signs of the transformation of a nation into a police state.

But it still remains true that Greece is a military autocracy and not a police state. Army leaders still hold the principal positions of power. Complaints are frequently made that the directives of senior civil servants can be cancelled on the instructions of a young lieutenant[12] and that local authorities are supervised by a military committee. The basis of power in Greece is 'the allegiance of a few hundred army officers. These men now command all the main military units, control the intelligence network, and hold headquarter jobs from which they can watch the actions of the generals. The government is holding on to power through martial law and the eyes and ears of the secret police and informers.'[13]

This deliberate monopolizing of all the main positions of power by the army accounts to some extent for Greece's failure to become a police state. The army has so far kept the police apparat, powerful though it has become, in a subordinate position, and has kept its own controls over the civil service and the judiciary, without abandoning their supervision entirely to police surveillance. And the critical factor has probably been that the army has prevented the police apparat from emerging as a unified force with the political police as its leader. The uniformed branch has been kept separate even although the criminal and political police have been closely associated. In the last resort the army has preferred to do its own policing, and no para-state armed police service outside military control has as yet emerged to rival the army's internal authority. This has been at the price, as one critic notes, of turning the army itself into a glorified but inglorious police force.[14]

These random reports suggest that today there is nothing specifically left wing or right wing about police states. They occur independently of the political philosophy of the state. They grow up when authoritarian philosophies meet resistance. They are created in reaction to a special kind of dissidence in society. In one sense, they are historical accidents. Joseph II did not set out to create a repressive system of government; he was simply afraid that his reforms would be sabotaged by the traditional classes, or his regime subverted by the Illuminati. Fouché did not create the circumstances in which his police state could flourish; he worked on the institutional and psychological foundations laid by the leaders of the French Revolution. Lenin did not foresee Beria, and, ambiguous as his vision of society was, it is unlikely that he and his comrades of the Revolution saw that their path to an ideal society led through 'endless labour camps, brigades of inmate-citizens, and barracks of mass education'. And if one is detached enough there is some pathos in Frank's complaint that 'any ethical relationship between the leadership of the State and its citizens is being totally destroyed'.

Furthermore, there is precious little evidence that civil servants, politicians, soldiers or professional policemen actually plan to transform an authoritarian regime into a modern or totalitarian police state, even when they accept the general principle of authoritarian government on the grounds that it solves acute political problems, or is the best way to protect society, or is the only vehicle for social improvement.

The modern police state is the counterpart to passion and idealism in politics. This idealism can take two forms, but it always originates in a desire to utilize the machinery of the state for the development of society and the improvement of individuals—whatever the terms 'improvement' and 'development' may mean in a particular context. The robust rejection by the common law countries in the nineteenth century of any of the institutions or theories of the police state was based as much on their determination to keep the sphere of politics clear of the sphere of morals, as it was on their fear of a strong executive. The beneficent and paternal legislation and administration in Germany during the nineteenth century provided the psychological, juristic and social bases on which Himmler could work.

The type of idealism which underlies the creation of police states comes from the conviction that man as a social animal is perfectible, an impatience at his waywardness and resistance to being improved, and the certainty that he ought to be forced to do so. The personal and political strength of reformers of this persuasion depends upon their ability to ignore two fairly obvious truths. First, that people do not necessarily become nicer by being compulsorily improved; and, second, that if you are concerned with unleashing the human spirit from bondage you have to be able to accept, as part of life, the vagaries and villainies of people, as well as their virtues.

The practical expression of this idealism takes one of two forms depending upon whether the notion of improvement is held by the government, or the opposition. When it is held by the government, the state machinery already in being is transformed into a positive mechanism for change. If its determination to proceed provokes extensive resistance, a democratic regime may develop authoritarian characteristics, or an authoritarian regime begin to take on the aspects of a modern police state. When, on the other hand, the notion of compulsory betterment is held by an internal opposition, this latter challenges the government on the grounds that there are political principles which ought to be imposed upon society; that the government is morally heinous in continuing to allow obvious social inequalities, or Jews or Communists or white men in office, or freedom of speech for others, or a private system of education. The list of what people can find morally heinous is endless.

The result of both these forms of idealism is the same: the government becomes engaged on the battlefield of political principles, and this introduces a new dimension into politics. All governments, if they are to survive, have to be able to cope with overt challenges to their authority. The introduction of a new tax has been a secular cause for many a bloody street battle. It is clearly understood on all sides that if a government fails to maintain its authority in the streets it will fall, and perhaps a whole regime with it. The role of the police services in these circumstances is also perfectly well known: to act as the government's troops to put down civil mutiny. This is accepted as the natural and normal role of the police in maintaining law and order.

This position changes when external acts of violence are used not to protest against specific measures, or to bring to public notice specific grievances, or to demand government alleviation of a social ill, but when such acts are an adjunct to, or an auxiliary form of attack upon, the fundamental political purposes that the government is determined to defend or advance. That is, the preconditions for a modern police state emerge when there is a deliberate, embracing, and concerted attempt to subvert the existing institutions and political principles of government. The modern police state is frequently a philosophical reaction as much as a political phenomenon.

The challenge of political principles, whether that of a government undertaking to change society, or of an opposition claiming to possess revealed truths, unleashes a special form of police contest. Whereas overt acts of hostility can be countered by the most traditional means of organized public force, attempts to subvert the intellectual and moral foundations of society pose a special police problem. In this situation one can never start a single conspiracy: a counter-conspiracy is inevitably mounted by the police apparat. And this is work for those most specialized in ferreting out danger, in moving secretly, in mounting the silent but unceasing watch on the foundations of society—the political police. The principles of such a service are fundamentally different from those of the normal civil and criminal police. The normal police services are concerned with objective breaches of the law, the written code, the formal evidence of public right and wrong. The political police look for subjective error, the spoken clue, the intercepted letter, the informal suspicion of private heresy. The normal police are the custodians of public behaviour; the political police the moral censors of private beliefs.

When such a battle is joined the necessary preconditions for a police state exist. When the regime emerges relatively unruffled by the attempts at internal opposition or subversion, and continues policies which commend themselves to the silent majority, the political police remain ubiquitous but quiescent, moralizing and watching but not governing, the quiet instrument of social control of the traditional police state. But if the challenge is brusque and unnerving, the political police become, as we have seen, the principal protective force in society, dominating the whole police apparat, and ultimately challenging for the role of determinant over the whole field of internal policy. When, in the last resort, the challenge of principles is so great, or the compulsive nature of the ideology so absorbing and compelling, the path is open to the totalitarian police state.

In sum, if one looks fairly at the history, the police state germinates in the seeds of self-evident truths, grows on the passion of thwarted ideals, and comes to fruition in the ashes of destroyed aspirations. Those who, claiming to fear them, involve the police in ideological conflict, sometimes, in their passion, forget the Bengali proverb: Where you fear to meet the tiger, dusk falls.

References

For reasons of economy I have restricted these notes to three matters: direct quotations; contentious points which may require supporting
evidence; works which are the only source of evidence for a particular
matter. Full names of authors and the titles of the works to which I refer will
be found in the bibliography.

1/The Origins of the Term

This chapter is based upon the works of Beidtel, Büsch, Emerson,
Epstein, Finer, Guarino, Jolowicz, Kunkel, Post, Ritter; the national dic-
tionaries of different countries, and in particular *La Grande Encyclopédie
Française*, the *Enciclipodia Italiana*, and the *Deutsche Lexicon*; and for the
linguistics Forcellini's *Totius Latinitatis Lexicon*, first published 1771, Ains-
worth's *Dictionary*, E. Huguet's *Dictionnaire de la Langue du Seizieme Siècle*,
Didier, Paris 1965, and P. Robert's *Dictionnaire de la Langue Française*, Littré,
Paris 1962.

2/The Traditional Police State

The most useful books for this chapter are those by Beidtel, Daudet
Epstein, Godechot, Huber, Jäger, Kretschmayer, Lévy, Madelin, Padover
and Tulard.

1 Quoted in Padover.
2 See Epstein, pp. 87–92.
3 Ibid.
4 Ibid., p. 94.
5 Ibid., p. 88.
6 Padover, pp. 132–3.
7 Quoted in Lévy.
8 Ibid.
9 Ibid.
10 Ibid.
11 Ibid.
12 Ibid.

3/The Police State in Transition

The most useful books for this chapter are those by Andrieux,
Augustin-Thierry, Chapman, Chaput de Saintonge, Daudet, Fosdick,
Gisquet, Huber, Jacob, Kretschmayer, de Laubadère, Payne, Raynaud and
Tulard.

1   Chaput de Saintonge, p. 6 ff.
2   Chapman, p. 84 ff., Jacob, p. 16.
3   Payne, p. 7.
4   Ibid., p. 267.
5   Ibid., p. 267.
6   Fosdick, p. 20.
7   Chapman, p. 32 ff.
8   Quoted in Chapman.
9   Chapman, p. 190 ff.
10   Fosdick, p. 350.
11   Ibid., p. 29.
11   Ibid., p. 29.
12   Ibid., p. 296.
13   Ibid., p. 83.

4/New Meanings of the Term

Radzinowicz is the authority for the first part of this chapter. I am greatly indebted to Mr. R. W. Burchfield, the editor of *The Oxford English Dictionary Supplement*, for his help in tracing the changing meaning of the term.

1   Radzinowicz, Introduction.
2   The original is in the McCord Museum, Quebec.

5/The Modern Police State

There is by now an enormous amount of literature on the creation and development of National Socialist Germany. The authors I have found particularly helpful are Buchheim, Broszat et al., Crankshaw, Delarue, Höhne, Kogon, Manvell and Fraenkel, Mommsen, Peterson, Phillips, Schellenberg, Schorn and Wheeler-Bennet.

1   Buchheim, in Broszat et al., p. 134.
2   Quoted in Finer.
3   Buchheim, in Broszat et al., p. 137.
4   Ibid., p. 135.
5   Quoted in Delarue.
6   Ibid.
7   Ibid.
8   Quoted by Buchheim, in Broszat et al.
9   Ibid., p. 35.
10   Buchheim, in Broszat et al., p. 143.

6/Police Methods

The most useful books for this chapter are those by Andrieux, Augustin-Thierry, Brown, Conquest, Fosdick, Raynaud, Wolin and Slusser.

1   *Times Law Report*, January 25, 1968.
2   *L'Espresso*, April 20, 1969.

3 Raynaud, p. 43.
4 Ibid., p. 45.
5 In carton number F712717.
6 Report to Parliament by the Minister of Defence, On. Tremelloni.
7 Ibid.

7/Police Psychology

The most helpful books for this chapter are the works of Balzac, and the studies by Brown, Conquest, Crankshaw, Delarue, Höhne, Lévy, Lifton, Manvell and Fraenkel, Schellenberg, Whyte, Wolin and Slusser.

1 S. Lipsett 'Politics of the Police', in *New Society*, March 6, 1969.
2 Whyte, pp. 138–9.
3 Ibid., p. 136.
4 Quoted in Lévy.
5 Quoted in Wolin and Slusser.
6 Lifton, p. 315.
7 See Brown, p. 286 ff.
8 Ibid., p. 285.
9 Wolin and Slusser.

8/The Totalitarian Polioo State

There is an enormous amount of literature relevant to this chapter. I have found the most useful books to be those by Buchheim, Broszat et al., Conquest, Crankshaw, Delarue, Höhne, Ionescu, Ionescu and Madariaga, Kogon, Manvell and Fraenkel, Mommsen, Nakano, Peterson, Schellenberg, Schorn, Wheeler-Bennet, and Wolin and Slusser.

1 Quoted by Buchheim, in Broszat et al.
2 Ibid.
3 Buchheim, in Broszat, p. 361.
4 Ionescu, p. 82.
5 Hume, *On the First Principles of Government*.
6 Ionescu, p. 84.
7 Ibid., p. 105.

9/Conclusion

For the central analysis contained in this chapter I have drawn widely upon a number of the leading newspapers, in particular on *The Times*, the London *Sunday Times*, the London *Telegraph* and *Sunday Telegraph*, the *Guardian, Le Monde, Il Corriere della Sera* and *La Stampa*.

1 Tsuneishi, pp. 32–3.
2 Ionescu and Madariaga, p. 165.
3 Ionescu, pp. 107 ff.
4 *Guardian*, June 30, 1969.
5 Clare Hollingworth in the *Daily Telegraph*, September 3, 1969.
6 *The Times*, July 1, 1969, and the *Daily Telegraph*, June 28, 1969.

7   *The Times*, October 27, 1969.
8   Ibid., November 20, 1969.
9   Ibid., July 15, 1967.
10 Ibid., June 30, 1969.
11 *The Times*, June 20, 1969, and the *Guardian*, August 19, 1969.
12 *Guardian*, October 4, 1969.
13 *The Economist*, October 25, 1969.
14 Peter Calvocoressi in *The Times*, October 16, 1969.

Bibliography

The principal bibliographical difficulty encountered in this study is that there are countless books relating in a general way to the topic, but virtually no single work devoted to close analysis. The police state has been a concept for two hundred years, but in all that time only a handful of books has appeared in any European language dealing simply with the police as a political institution. This meant that in order to trace the concept from its origins to the present day I have had to dabble in the fields of history, linguistics, comparative jurisprudence, psychology, biography, administrative law and contemporary political institutions. In these circumstances I have made no effort to list all the books which have provided me with hints, allusions and oblique suggestions. Each chapter is an amalgam of material from different sources, and I have therefore restricted the bibliography to those books which have referred centrally to my subject, and which have provided concrete evidence which I have used directly.

ANDRIEUX, L., *Souvenirs d'un Préfet de Police*, Rouff, Paris 1885, 2 vols.

ASENJO, E. JIMENEZ, *Ley de Orden Publico de 30 de julio de 1959*, Instituto de Estudios Politicos, Madrid 1961.

AUGUSTIN-THIERRY, GILBERT, *Conspirateurs et Gens de Police*, Armand Colin, Paris 1903.

BEIDTEL, I., *Geschichte der Östereichischen Staatsverwaltung 1740–1848*, Vol I 1740–92. Huber, Innsbruck 1896.

BROWN, J. A. C., *Techniques of Persuasion: from Propaganda to Brainwashing*, Penguin, Harmondsworth 1963.

BUCHHEIM, HANS, *The Third Reich: Its beginnings, its development, its end.* Kösel-Verlag, Munich 1961.

BROSZAT, MARTIN; BUCHHEIM, HANS; JACOBSEN, HANS-ADOLF; KRAUSNICK, HELMUT, *Anatomy of the SS State*, introduction by Elizabeth Wiskemann, Collins 1968.

BÜSCH, OTTO, *Militärsystem und Sozialleben im Alten Preussen 1713–1807*, de Gruyter, Berlin 1962.

CATALDI, G., *Le Legislazioni Speciali*, Zanichelli, Bologna 1956.

CHAPMAN, BRIAN, *The Profession of Government*, Allen & Unwin, London, 1960.

CHAPUT DE SAINTONGE, R. A., *Public Administration in Germany*, Weidenfeld & Nicolson, London 1961.

CONQUEST, ROBERT, *The Soviet Police System*, Bodley Head, London 1968.

CRANKSHAW, EDWARD, *Gestapo: Instrument of Tyranny*, New English Library, London 1966.

DAUDET, ERNEST, *La Police Politique: chronique des temps de la Restauration 1815-1820*, Librairie Plon, Paris 1912.

DELARUE, JACQUES, *The History of the Gestapo*, trans. by Mervyn Savill, Corgi, London 1966.

EMERSON, R., *State and Sovereignty in Modern Germany*, Yale University Press, New Haven 1928.

EPSTEIN, KLAUS, *The Genesis of German Conservatism*, Princeton University Press, Princeton 1966.

FINER, H., *The Theory and Practice of Modern Government*, 2 vols., Methuen, London 1931.

FOSDICK, R., *European Police Systems*, first published 1915, rep. 1969.

GISQUET, M., *Mémoires*, 2 vols., Paris 1841.

GODECHOT, J., *Les Institutions de la France sous la Révolution et l'Empire*, P.U.F., Paris 1951.

GUARINO, ANTONIO, *Storia del Diritto Romano*, Jovene, Naples 1969.

HÖHNE, HEINZ, *The Order of the Death's Head*, trans. by Richard Barry. Secker & Warburg, London 1969.

HUBER, ERNST, *Deutsche Verfassungsgeschichte seit 1789*, 4 vols., Kohlhammer Verlag, Stuttgart 1960.

IONESCU, GHITA, *The Politics of the European Communist States*, Weidenfeld & Nicolson, London 1968.

IONESCU, GHITA and DE MADARIAGA, I., *Opposition: past and present of a political institution*, Watts, London 1968.

IRIBARNE, M. FRAGA, *General Introduction to Spanish Law*. Publicaciones Españolas, Madrid 1967.

JACOB, HERBERT, *German administration since Bismarck: central authority versus local autonomy*, Yale University Press, New Haven 1963.

JÄGER, A., *Kaiser Josef II und Leopold II: Reform und Gegenreform 1780–92*, Vienna 1867.

JOLOWICZ, H. F., *Historical Introduction to the Study of Roman Law*, Cambridge University Press, Cambridge 1952.

KOGON, EUGEN, *Der SS-Staat*, Europaischer Verlagsanstalt 1965.

KRETSCHMAYER, HEINRICH, *Die Österreichische Zentralverwaltung*, Abteilung II Adolf Holzhausens, Vienna 1938.

KUNKEL, W., *Roman Legal and Constitutional History*, trans. by J. M. Kelly Oxford University Press, London 1966.

DE LAUBADÈRE, A., *Traité Elémentaire de Droit Administratif*, Paris 1965.

LÉVY, YVES, "Police and Policy", *Government and Opposition*, Sept. 1966.

LIFTON, R. J., *Thought Reform and the Psychology of Totalitarianism: a study of brainwashing in China*, Penguin, Harmondsworth 1966.

MADELIN, LOUIS, *Histoire du Consulat et de l'Empire*, Hachette, Paris 1945.

MANVELL, R. and FRAENKEL, H., *Heinrich Himmler*, Heinemann, London 1965.

MOMMSEN, HANS, *Beamtentum im Dritten Reich*, Deutsche Verlagsanstalt, Stuttgart 1966.

NAKANO, T., *The Ordinance Power of the Japanese Emperor*, Johns Hopkins, Baltimore 1922.

PADOVER, S. K., *The Revolutionary Emperor: Joseph II of Austria*, Eyre & Spottiswoode, London 1967.

PAYNE, HOWARD C., *The Police State of Louis Napoleon Bonaparte 1851–1860*, University of Washington Press, Seattle 1966.

PETERSON, E. N., *The Limits of Hitler's Power*, Princeton University Press, Princeton 1969.

PHILLIPS, PETER, *The Tragedy of Nazi Germany*, Routledge & Kegan Paul, London 1969.

POST, G., *Studies in Mediaeval Legal Thought: Public Law and the State, 1100–1322*, Princeton University Press, Princeton 1969.

RADZINOWICZ, LEON, *A History of English Criminal Law and its Administration*, Vol. 3, Stevens & Sons, London 1956.

RAYNAUD, E., *Souvenirs de Police* and *La vie intime des commissariats*, Payot, Paris 1926.

RITTER, GERHARD, *Frederick the Great: an historical profile*, trans. by P. Paret, Eyre & Spottiswoode, London 1968.

SCHELLENBERG, WALTER, *Schellenberg*, ed. and trans. by Louis Hagen, intro. by Alan Bullock, Mayflower, London 1965.

SCHORN, HUBERT, *Der Richter im Dritten Reich: Geschichte und Dokumente*, Klostermann, Frankfurt a-M. 1959.

TSUNEISHI, WARREN M., *Japanese Political Style*, Harper & Row, New York 1966.

THIARD, J., *Le Préfecture de Police sous la Monarchie de Juillet*, Imprimerie Municipale, Paris 1904.

WATSON, BURTON (trans. and ed.), *Han Fei Tzu*, Columbia University Press, New York 1964.

WHEELER-BENNET, J., *The Nemesis of Power: the German Army in Politics 1918–1945*, Macmillan, London 1953.

WHYTE, WILLIAM FOOTE, *Street Corner Society: the social structure of an Italian slum*, University of Chicago Press, Chicago 1943.

WOLIN, S. and SLUSSER, ROBERT, *The Soviet Secret Police*, Praeger, New York 1957.

Index